GLORY

WHERE ATMOSPHERES COLLIDE

GLORY
WHERE ATMOSPHERES COLLIDE

By
Dr. Sherlock Bally

Logos to Rhema Publishing
11063-D South Memorial Drive # 346
Tulsa, OK 74133

*Published in the
United States of America by*

Susan K. Reidel
Logos to Rhema Publishing
11063-D South Memorial Drive # 346
Tulsa, OK 74133
(918) 606-5346

CONTENTS

Chapter 1

Glory–God's Dimension

John 17 verses 1 to 4 are a record of the prayer that Jesus prayed for His people. Matthew 6 is not the Lord's Prayer as is often thought; it is the disciples' prayer since this was the way that Jesus wanted the disciples to pray. It was actually direction to effectual prayer. The Lord's Prayer is found in John 17. It is the prayer that Jesus specifically prayed for His children. It is an amazing thought to contemplate, that over 2,000 years ago, Jesus, who knows past, present and future, prayed a prayer for you. He who knows things about you that you don't even know about yourself, He prayed for you. He who sees the entire plan, purpose and picture of your life, He prayed a prayer for you. Because of this fact, it is imperative that you understand this prayer. It is of the utmost importance that you see the details of this prayer for in it lies a spiritual universe of supernatural revelation. His prayer for you does involve His understanding of your need, your trials, your past, present and your future. We, therefore, must have a personal revelation of the contents of this prayer so that we can receive an internal revelation of the mind of Christ in relation to life and living.

It is impossible in this book to give a full treatment of this prayer so we shall deal with one predominant point that is the substance of the prayer. Generally speaking, though, the elements of this prayer demonstrate amazing truths that are extremely relevant to our lives today. In more than one place, the Lord speaks of His people being one so that the world would know that God, the Father had sent Him. Today the fragmentation of the church is very visible. Lives are fractured by disunity and Christians are divided by doctrine, by traditions, by liturgy and by opinion. Even though we are united by Absolute truths, yet so many have let other things of lesser importance bring disunity. Herod and Pilate were enemies but they became friends to crucify Jesus. Iran and Syria were enemies but became friends to attack Israel. China and Russia were enemies but they became friends because of expansionism. Enemies in the world have cast aside their bigotries and formed unholy alliances to see their godless purposes achieved. Yet Christians have not been able to come together, to cast aside their disagreements so that the purpose of the harvest can be expedited.

Jesus prayed that we would be one as He and the Father are one. This contains a world of revelation but this point is not the object of this book although Biblical teaching of oneness and unity is of paramount importance to the body of Christ. The attack of the enemy on the unity of the body testifies to his fear of this unity. The mention of this in His prayer in John 17 is a great reminder of how important unity is to the body of Christ.

In this prayer, one of the frequently mentioned things is the world. Jesus was filled with the Heaven-sent purpose that the world be impacted by His people. God's vision is more than local or even regional. It is global. There is a vital need in the church today, for a deeper understanding of this. So many churches have lost touch with God's purpose and have locked themselves in the prison of personal agendas. Because of this, much of the effort of church life has to do with maintaining a programme instead of reaching out to touch the world. There is a vital need for the church to rediscover its reason for being and to walk in its mission which is - touching the world.

So many have become introverted and their vision has focussed on personal things - their programmes, their buildings, their plans have become their world. They say essentially, "This parish is my world," when they should say, "This world is my parish." So much effort is centred on their comfort, their lifestyle, their dream, so that they have become complacent and irrelevant. There is little emphasis on the Word, winning the lost, reaching the region and impacting the community. This infatuation with self, this enamourment with the physical, this absorption with material things have all combined to rock many to sleep in the lap of Delilah. In the light of this, it is evident that the prayer that Jesus prayed over 2000 years ago is of vital relevance to the church today.

As said before, even thought the elements of the prayer are of enormous importance, they are not the emphasis of this work. I find in this prayer, though, a revelation that is of such Heavenly importance that if it is understood and grasped, transformation is inevitable. This prayer gives a pattern for the present, perspective for the future and an infusion of revelation that will equip you for any eventuality of life. Remember, it is the prayer that Jesus prayed. When trial or trauma befalls you, the prayer of the Pastor or the prayer of the intercessors is solicited. This is acceptable practice. But how does it make you feel to know that Jesus, the Son of God, Jesus, your Saviour and Lord prayed a prayer for you. Hallelujah! What a thought! So whereas we will be emphasizing one element of this prayer, I would recommend that you do a study of the entire prayer as it is recorded in John 17.

By now, you must be wondering what the predominant emphasis of this book is. So here we go. In this prayer that takes up such a small space, Jesus talked pointedly twice, about one thing. He said, "Father, the glory that you have given me, I give to them." Then He said, "I pray that they behold my glory." Jesus thought this to be so important that twice in three verses, He repeated Himself concerning Glory. No greater testimony can be given to the vital importance of Glory than the repetition of our Lord in these verses. He could have prayed for us to receive any number of things, but He didn't. His prayer was concerning Glory.

Let us examine our requests or petitions in prayer. Many pray for healing, deliverance, supply, salvation of the home, increase in wisdom and a vast array of things. These things are in themselves, worthy prayers and we must continue in prayer and intercession. But Jesus did not prayer for all these things. Instead, He prayed that we would receive Glory. There are many elements of Glory; there are different manifestations of Glory all of which I will address in future chapters.

So if Jesus knows that we will need healing, deliverance, salvation and so many other things, why did He pray that we would have an encounter with Glory?

John 1:14 says, "...*And we beheld His glory ...full of grace and truth.*"

Grace and truth in themselves are not glory. Grace and truth are constituent elements of Glory. Glory is a dimension, it is God's dimension; it is the Heavenly dimension. Healing, deliverance, supply are not Glory. They are only are a part of Glory. **Glory is the Heavenly whole; it is the complete dimension.** Within this Heavenly dimension of Glory is everything that we need. All God-operations, all God-manifestations are elements that fill His dimension of Glory. So when the Glory of God abides, when we encounter that Glory and live in that Glory, all that we really need is in that dimension. One touch of the Glory of God brings Heaven to earth. Instead of having an isolated manifestation of Glory, Our Lord wants us to live in and walk in the dimension of Glory.

NOT JUST MANIFESTATION BUT DIMENSION.

So many have decided that the Glory of God is manifested in certain ways. So that for many, these manifestations are the only ways that Glory can be seen. We must note carefully that Glory is not pre-eminently a manifestation but a dimension. It is Heaven's dimension. It is God's dimension. God is saying that He wants you to live in a Heavenly dimension while you are on earth. Whereas manifestation is spasmodic, dimension can be lived in perpetually. Many have chosen the "off and on" of manifestation instead of "the day to day" of dimension. I do not decry manifestation, but if the manifestation, regardless of how powerful or unusual does not lead to a life- increase, a life-enduement, then we have fallen woefully short. God's will is not living in a touch of His power intermittently, but to live in His Glory.

You will find later in this book, terms like "filled with Glory,' walking in Glory," "changed by His Glory," "looking through His Glory." The good must not become the enemy of the best. Never have so many taken so little from the God who has so much. A little manifestation may satisfy my outer man, but I cannot be satisfied with the crashing wave that cracks like thunder and then disappears into a foamy mass. There is a current that draws me in that has astonishing power. Whenever you walk in this dimension, the inevitable consequence will be manifestation. When the children of Israel followed the pillar of cloud and fire, this was a manifestation of the Glory of God. It was when God sent His dimension that the manifestation came. The manifestation was a physical expression of God's dimension. We must get to the place where we walk in God's dimension or God's realm where we will see His manifestations. To dwell on what you see, to live to satisfy the eye-gate, to live to titillate emotion is to rob you of your greatest encounter. There is a realm of Heavenly operation that God has for us today. There is a dimension of Heaven that God has given to those who serve Him. "Thy kingdom come, Thy will be done on earth as it is in Heaven." God's will is that Heaven reaches your body before your body reaches Heaven. There is a Heavenly work appointed to those who would receive it. God is more willing to give it than you are to receive it.

WALKING IN THE GLORY DIMENSION

Hebrews 6: 4-6 says: *"For it is impossible for those who were once enlightened, and have*

tasted of the heavenly gift, and were made par-
takers of the Holy Ghost,
   And have tasted the good word of God, and
the powers of the world to come,
   If they shall fall away, to renew them again
unto repentance; seeing they crucify to them-
selves the Son of God afresh, and put him to an
open shame."

According to this scripture, we have been enlightened. God's Heavenly light has illuminated our lives and the darkness that benighted us, has disappeared. We have also tasted of the Heavenly gift of salvation. I was dead but now I am alive. We have been made partakers of the Heavenly nature and have tasted the good Word of God. These are all powerful infusions that have taken place because of the precious gift of salvation. Then come the words of the Spiritual Revolution. "We have tasted the powers of the world to come." Heaven, the world to come, has powers that Almighty God wants us to taste today. The heart of God is that whatever there is in Heaven is destined to become yours. It is described as powers. Yes the powers of the world to come can become yours today. Is it possible that Almighty God is saying that I am ready to share with you, the dimension in which I live?

What is earth dimension?

1John 2:15-17 says, *"Love not the world neither the things that are in the world. If any man love the world, the love of the Father is not in him.*

16. For all that is in the world, the lust of the flesh, and the lust of the eyes, and the pride of life, is not of the Father, but is of the world.

17. And the world passeth away, and the lust thererof: but he that doeth the will of God abideth forever."

All that is in the world, no matter how tinsel-covered it seems, is filled with the lust of the flesh, lust of the eyes and the pride of life. The lust of the flesh is passion, the lust of the eyes is possession, the pride of life is position. Passion, possession and position are the renegade trio that wreaks havoc over a Godless world. This produces doubts, fear, unbelief, rebellion and trauma. God is saying that His will is that your life be filled with the Heavenly dimension of Glory. I John 5:19 says, *"And we know that we are of God, and the whole world lieth in wickedness."*

The whole world "lieth" in the evil one so it is filled with wickedness. I am in the world but not of the world so although my body is here, my roots are in Heaven. There is a choice that must be made. Will you walk in the dimension of earth that produces all the chaos and confusion that you see? Or will you walk in the Heaven-sent supernatural dimension of Glory that God has given? I don't just want His glory at the beginning or at the end. I want to walk in that Glory for the entire journey.

Two men went into a bar and stayed there for 5 hours ingesting smoke and "liquoring up" their lives. They came outside and one said to the other, "What is that I smell?" the other replied, "Fresh air, stupid!" They had become so accustomed to foul air that they thought it strange when they smelled fresh air. There are so many Christians that have lived below their privileges, that have ingested the foul air of doubt, oppression and depression, that now a supernatural dimension is open, they are impeded by astonishment.

Is there really a victorious life? Is there really a dimension of Glory? Does God love me enough to give me this privilege? Have I lived so long in bondage, can I ever rise? Yes it is time to walk. There is a Heaven-sent dimension that God has ordained for you. But it necessitates your movement. You have been immobilized long enough and today marks a new walk, a new path, a new engagement.

"THE GLORY YOU HAVE GIVEN ME, I HAVE GIVEN THEM."

This is one of the most illuminating verses in the Bible. Jesus is saying that the Glory that God gave Him, He has given to His people. This verse must be read over and over until it really becomes substance to us. The Glory that God gave to Jesus, Jesus has given to us. If this is so, and it is, then where is this Glory? When you look at a Christian today, can you say, I see the Glory of the Lord? In many cases I see frustration, fear, discouragement, oppression. Where is the Glory? I submit to you that Jesus has given the Glory but many in the household of faith have not received the Glory. There is something that has hindered so many from receiving this Glory that Jesus said that He gave. What is the thing that has hindered so many from receiving the dimension of Heaven? I submit to you that it is the dimension of earth - the lust of the flesh, the lust of the eyes and the pride of life that have been injected into the lives of the children of God. There is the lust of the flesh - passion - that causes us to love what we should hate and hate what we should love. There is the displacing of Godly priorities with selfish, carnal, worldly priorities. The utter infatuation with fleshly things has created severe spiritual reversals in the lives of

Christians. The strewn wreckage of families, marriages, relationships with children, a society that is on the moral precipice, all reflect the lust of the flesh.

The lust of the eyes is possession. Many have mortgaged their future for their present. The bottomless pit of greed has dealt a pulverizing blow of debt, the lustful gaze of the coveting soul drives them to want to possess things. They are possessed by things so life revolves around their drive to thrive.

The pride of life represents position and there are so many that will climb the ladder of position at the expense of everything to ascend to a place of superior privilege. Sounds like Isaiah 14 and Lucifer's five "I wills," that got Him kicked out of Heaven. Look around and see the havoc that has been wreaked on lives because of this Godless dimension. To think that someone will forfeit God's dimension to live in this putrefying dimension of earth, defies imagination.

These are the things that hinder the reception of the gift of Glory. Esau's inheritance sold for some stew that showed utter disregard and disrespect for the birthright blessing! Samson's hair cut and his binding, grinding and blinding! Please do not sell your future for your present. Do not be so enamoured with what you see that you forfeit what you can't see. Break this hold of the world! Bust this crust that has formed a shell around you. Be loosed from the graveclothes that have bound you. If you do what you can, God will do what you can't. God will not do the possible! There is an amazing Heavenly dimension that Jesus prayed that we would receive. He has already given this gift of Glory and now it must be received. May all hindrances to the reception of this Heavenly Glory, no matter, how cherished, how enamoured we are, how entangled we might be, may they be obliterated by purposeful and deliberate action, **TODAY!!!!!!!!!!!!!!**

CHAPTER 1

Summary

1. In the Lord's Prayer of John 17, Jesus emphasized Glory.

2. Along with His emphasis on Glory, is His emphasis to touch the world.

3. Glory is not manifestation but it is God's dimension.

4. It is the will of God for you to live in Heaven's dimension here on earth.

5. This Glory has already been given to you by Jesus.

6. The challenge is not on the giving end but on the receiving end.

All hindrances to receiving His Glory must be eliminated.

Chapter 2

ATMOSPHERES:
When Atmospheres Collide:

Rev 21:23 states:
"And the city had no need of the sun, either of the moon, to shine in it: for the glory of God did lighten it and the Lamb is the light thereof."

Heaven has no need for sun or moon to shine in it for the Glory of God lights up the city. The Glory of God that is God's dimension, has the power to light up all of the New Jerusalem. That is a thought about dimension producing manifestation at its highest level. To add to this, Jesus said that that Glory He has given to us: the same Glory that lights up Heaven is the same Glory that Jesus gave to us. So we are correct in saying that Heaven's atmosphere is the atmosphere of Glory and that there is no primary Glory for Heaven and secondary Glory for earth. It is a revolutionary thought that this Heavenly Glory is given to God's people here on earth.

As I said before, the atmosphere of earth is filled with wickedness, lust, oppression. Living in the dimension of earth connects us to this atmosphere. In turn that atmosphere creates a reality and that is manifested in the reality that exists in the life of the people. Satan is the prince of the power of the air, of the atmosphere. That atmosphere is satanically charged and filled to the extent that there are some places that you visit and you feel the atmosphere's heaviness. Everything that is in the world is inebriated by this air, this atmosphere. It is not the will of God that His people whom He has delivered from the kingdom of darkness be dominated and filled with that satanic atmosphere. If God has the power to light up an entire city eternally through His Glory, then the potential for supernatural breakthrough is unquestionable. God will not take you out of sin for sin to dominate you. He will not leave you to the whims and fancies of a satanically influenced system. When your child was born, did you leave the newborn baby outdoors for the atmosphere of winter to take charge? Did you leave the child unfed, unclothed and unprepared? No you did just the opposite. You loved, nurtured, nourished, embraced and protected that child. If human love and human parenting will protect and preserve, how much more will Almighty God who is the Heavenly Father, protect and preserve you. If you would not allow your children to be overtaken by attacks that you can prevent, why can't we understand that Our Father in Heaven will defend us.

Luke11:13 says,
"If you then being evil, know how to give good gifts to your children, how much more will your Heavenly Father...."

Almighty God with more love, more compassion and more ability will bless you and keep you.

THE ATMOSPHERE OF HEAVEN

All through the Bible, there is evidence of the atmosphere of Heaven or the Glory of God. The Ark of the Covenant in the Holy of Holies was where the Glory came and settled. The pillars of fire and of cloud were manifestations of Glory. When the temple was dedicated, the Glory of God filled the building. Isaiah saw the glory of God as His train filled the temple. In the Old Testament, it became increasingly evident that God wanted His people to have an encounter with His Glory. Once the ark which represented the Glory of God was with them, no enemy had the power to defeat them. You must know that God wants you to walk and live in the Glory. Whenever enemies came in contact with that Glory, they were blinded or destroyed or they killed themselves. Think for a moment of what would happen if the atmosphere of Heaven collided with the atmosphere of earth. The Glory of God will torpedo the pressure of the earthly atmosphere. If you are under the influence of the atmosphere of earth, Almighty God is about to show you the power of His Glory.

There are so many who pray about the problems that surround them, and in itself that is not an incorrect focus. However consider what would happen if you prayed about your atmosphere. If your atmosphere is filled with the atmosphere of Heaven, then nothing around you would have the power to imprison you. Think with me for a moment. Paul and Silas are in prison. They are in the inner prison chained in stocks. The prison is a dark, windowless room and they are surrounded by the atmosphere of bondage. However, at midnight they begin to praise God and suddenly there is a Heavenly intervention. The atmosphere of their life was not decided by the reality that was around them. When they began to praise, there was a manifestation of Heaven and it was a sudden manifestation. The foundation of the prison was shaken, all the doors were opened, a light shone, the jailer was about to kill himself. In the same way, God will shake the foundations of your prison,

He will open all the doors, bands will be loosed and His light will shine. Talk about atmospheres colliding!! The jailer lost power over his own jail when God's Glory shone into that dark corner of the universe.

If who is about you is in you, then what's around you cannot kill you. There is a Heavenly atmosphere called Glory that is available to you right now and whatever the earth has produced to afflict you or oppress you, its time of domination is over.

On the day of Pentecost which was the birthday of the church, there are some elements that were present that will seem very familiar to you. First, the disciples were in one accord and in one place so they were in unity. Next, fire and wind came among them. Next the world was impacted and the people that were in attendance saw the demonstration of God's power. These are the elements that were all in the prayer of Jesus in John 17. The atmosphere of Heaven filled the Upper Room so men were transformed by the power of God. Before Pentecost, they were hiding form Caesar's throne: after Pentecost, they were shaking Caesar's throne. God's dimension brought a reality that transformed the reality around them. I submit that we should not be symptomatic believers responding to every symptom that we see. We should be asking God to change our atmosphere and that changed atmosphere will change our reality. The disciples shook an empire and even though the Roman Empire launched one of the most violent campaigns against the church, the church spread and grew. The blood of the martyrs became the seed of the church. No circumstantial pressure has the ability to destroy you if your life is filled with God in His supernatural dimension of Glory.

SMOKE

There are many instances in the Old Testament when the Glory of God fell and the room was filled with smoke, at times, a cloud. Consider the priests in the Holy Place and the Holy of Holies. It is said that the smoke became so thick that the priest was unable to see his own hands. The thought is where the Glory of God is, there must be no flesh, and flesh must not be seen. Even the seraphim around the throne of God, hid their faces in the presence of the ALMIGHTY. The application is that in the presence of God, in the midst of His Glory, our faces must be hidden and only His face must be seen. If we can get rid of the showiness of the "face" in the church then the emphasis on the face of God would increase and an absolute outpouring of His power would follow.

Around the throne of God, the Glory of God is seen and in the midst of that Glory, the 24 elders speak of the worthiness of God. The 4 living creatures cry, "Holy, Holy, Holy." When the Glory of God moves us, when this Heavenly dimension comes in, the atmosphere is changed and charged and all that has to do with the earth becomes subservient in the midst of His Majesty. I am convinced by the abundance of scriptures, that it is the will of God to manifest that Heavenly dimension in this earthly life.

1 Corinthians 2:9 says, *"Eye hath not seen, nor ear heard, neither hath it entered into the heart of man, the things which God hath prepared for them that love Him"*

The scripture validates important considerations. Firstly God has prepared certain things for His children that are so profound in their Heavenly orientation that eyes have not seen nor have ears heard. The Scripture continues by saying, "Neither hath it entered into the heart of man the things that God has prepared..." Even the heart of man with all its wisdom and the mind with all its imagination cannot comprehend these things that God has prepared. The next verse goes on to say, "But God has revealed them to us now by His Spirit. There is a revelation of Heavenly things prepared by God that is given here, now, today, here on earth. Hebrews 6:5 talks about "...the powers of the age to come." 1 Corinthians 2 speaks of the things that God has prepared. In talking about the Heavenly dimension, we also note that the plural form of speech is employed: "the powers," "the things." This dimension of Heaven, this Glory cannot be communicated in one act or one experience. This Glory is so infinite that it will take many infusions of the Holy Spirit to even begin to understand His Glory.

THE ARK AND THE HOLY OF HOLIES

The Outer Court, the Holy Place and the Holy of Holies all had immense significance to the Israelites. However, the entire journey through the Tabernacle had the ultimate aim of getting to the Holy of Holies. As you entered the Outer Court, there was the brazen altar and the brazen laver. One represented cleansing by blood: the other represented cleansing by water. One represented internal cleansing: the other represented external cleansing. Now that the cleansing aspect was finished, the journey could continue to the Holy Place. No cleansing would mean no advancement to the Holy Place.

Here in the Holy Place, there were 3 articles: the Table of Shewbread, the Golden Lampstand and the Altar of Incense. One represented Jesus as the bread of life, our sustenance; the Lampstand represented the Holy Spirit, the oil that lightens up your life; and the Altar of Incense represented our prayer and praise. This brings us to the number 5: 2 articles in the Outer Court plus 3 articles in the Holy of Holies. Five is the number of grace so it is correct to say that the Holy Place represented the place of grace. However the ultimate aim of Almighty God was to get the priest to the Holy of Holies. Here is where the Glory of God fell and this reflected the number 7 representing fullness and completion. The number is used numerous times in the Bible to signify this fullness and completion. In the Book of Revelation, there are 7 candlestands which are the 7 churches which also symbolize the complete church age with a complete message. There are 7 stars which represent the pastors of these churches. There are 7 spirits symbolizing the full and complete move of the Holy Spirit.

In the book of Genesis, there are 7 days of creation, including God's rest day all combining to symbolize this work of creative completion. In Joshua 6, there is the record of the crumbling walls at

Jericho. They surrounded the city for 7 days and 7 priests with 7 trumpeters on the 7th day blew the trumpets 7 times. On the last day they walked around the city 7 times, then the walls came tumbling down. In the time of Pharaoh, there was famine for 7 years and with the emergence of Joseph, they became 7 years of abundance. Naaman dipped 7 times in the Jordan River and there was the complete work of healing. There are many, many more instances of this number 7 being the number of fullness and completion and the complete move of God.

This complete move of the Almighty was the descent of His Glory. Now the plan was to go from 5 to 7 or from grace in the Holy Place to Glory in the Holy of Holies. Grace was only the entrance to lead to Glory. Grace was never the end, but the means to the end. Grace is a wonderful thing but it always leads to Glory. To stop at number 5 or to stop at the place of grace regardless of how wonderful it is, is to be deprived of God's ultimate descent. What percentage of the church is at number 5 and has never entered into number 7? How many are living in grace but have never entered the place of Glory. Paul says, "Shall we continue in sin that grace may abound? Shall we sin from Monday to Saturday, live in fleshly gratification and then come on Sunday morning pleading for grace to cover and deliver? Spiritual life must be more than a repetitive cycle of blessing and blasting, bondage and deliverance, sin and cleansing. If who is above you is in you, then what's around you cannot dominate you. He who is above all and in all, is infinitely more powerful than all the forces of the enemy combined. Shall we live in this cycle repeating the same mistakes until death? God has a greater and more glorious plan for our lives.

Now between the numbers 5 and 7, there is the number 6. Between the Holy Place and the Holy of Holies, there was the veil. Paul says the veil represents my flesh and of course 6 is the number of man. In order to get to where the Glory is, the veil must be pulled down. In more direct terms, the flesh must be pulled down. At both ends of this veil, there were 2 cherubim and it was as though they were saying, the entrance into this place was forbidden. I don't know what stares you in the face on a daily basis prohibiting you from entry. I do not know what manifestation of flesh mocks you and tells you that there will never be a life filled with Glory. Whether it is something in the past, something that is genetically inherited or a cherished indulgence of a fortified stronghold, today Almighty God beckons you to come into the Holy of Holies where His Glory is. When Jesus died, this veil was torn form the top to the bottom. Human effort would tear it form the bottom to the top but when God pulled it down, no part of it was left standing. This flesh, this personal veil, can be torn down by the application of the work of the Cross. You have been made a temple to house the Glory of God and this is your ultimate destiny.

Let me show you the difference between the Holy Place and the Holy of Holies. In the Holy Place, someone has to put out the bread, someone has to put out the oil and someone has to put the incense and the coal where they should be placed. In the Holy of Holies, it is God and God alone. No man has his print in this Holy Place. Only the Glory of God is seen. There are so many that live lives that are cyclical. The church has become the 1 day (in many cases) of blessing, encouragement and edification. That spirit, that blessing does not transcend into their lives from Monday to Saturday. Because of this, many Christians seem disconnected from the realm of blessing and deliverance so that the Monday to Saturday life is filled with trauma, trial and trepidation. This realm that they walk in is not God's plan and if lives are to be consistent, walking in God's realm is imperative.

In the Holy of Holies, the impact would touch the entire nation of Israel. Once again, in the realm of Glory, we see the world view that God's plan is to touch the nations and the world. Here in the Holy of

Holies, it was not about the priest, the sacrifice, even though they were important, the experience was about the descent of the Glory of God. This Glory fell on the Day of Atonement or Yom Kippur. The entire nation would have witnessed and been in a state of awe at this Glory cloud called the Shekinah.

Grace, we must agree is a most wonderful gift from God. One of its meanings is:

God's **R**iches **A**t **C**hrist's **E**xpense.

Grace is of vital importance to the child of God but it is not the place that I terminate my journey. Grace leads to Glory and here in the dimension of Glory, I find my true destiny. It is within our power to apply the work of the Cross by faith and pull down this veil of flesh. Whatever has stopped you from entering into the dimension of Glory, whatever has stopped you from entering into your truest destiny while on earth will be pulled down by the application of the work of the Cross. Paul said that we should mortify the deeds of our body which represents purposeful, deliberate action to bring to nought the working of the flesh. Why haven't more people entered into this God-given, God-provided dimension of Glory? It is because the veil is erected, the fleshly hindrance remains standing, the hands of the flesh point to you and say no entrance. To indulge any form of flesh, no matter how carnally gratifying, is an indictment on your spiritual life. To forfeit the life that is filled with Heaven's Glory for a life filled with compromise is to settle for a body of death.

The devil will do all he can, erect any stronghold, place any hindrance, build any prison to obstruct your path to glory. It is here in the place of Glory, living this life of Glory, flowing in the dimension of this Glory that you have power and authority over all the power of the enemy. In this dimension of Glory, the devil has no power and no ability to operate. Satan needs the atmosphere of wickedness to fulfil his diabolical plans. Remember in Isaiah 14, Lucifer aspired to have that glory and attempted to supplant the Almighty and so He was swiftly and summarily kicked out of Heaven. When Almighty God gave you the gift of Glory, the dimension of Glory, it brought a panic in the domain of Satan. You now have access to something that he has no ability to overcome. There is nothing in the devil's pathetic, weakened kingdom that can short circuit Glory. When he was Lucifer, he knew that Glory, that dimension and what that atmosphere was. He was the angel that was close to the throne. The aspiration to get that throne by rebellion, to defy the authority of God, to take the position of pride and arrogance began his demise. Because of his understanding of what this dimension of Glory is and what it does, he will do all he can to stop you from flowing in that realm but he has no way of stopping Glory, of changing the dimension of Glory or stopping its atmosphere from bringing supernatural manifestation. Since he cannot stop Glory, his attempt is to stop you. To stop you from entrance into that dimension, to stop you from living in its atmosphere and experiencing the manifestation that Glory brings. The attack of the enemy to stop you form entering in, of flowing with and living in this atmosphere, testifies to his fear of the Glory.

It seems incomprehensible that God's people would know so little about Glory. We speak of His kingdom coming and His presence with us, yet so many have never understood the possibility of living in the Glory of God. Many have allowed things of little importance, things veneered with fleshliness, attitudes that are reflections of pride and arrogance, to stop them. They have settled for the carnal stew instead of the Heavenly Glory. Their earthbound desires have robbed them of the Heavenly dimension. Whenever I see pride and arrogance in Christians, I become very concerned about their lives. This is that Luciferian inheritance that will cause them to be kicked out of the realm of blessing.

I ask that you understand the wonderful life that God has provided for you while you live on earth. I ask that you see that you do not have to be pulverized by the atmosphere of chaos and defeat. I ask that you behold this dimension of Glory that you can walk in and live in right now. Then I ask that you violently pull down with the weapons of your warfare, any wall, hindrance, veil that will stop you from entrance. This is your moment, your new season, your God-appointed destiny.

Seize it, walk in it and in God's dimension of Glory!!!

CHAPTER 2

Summary

1. The atmosphere of Heaven is Glory.

2. The atmosphere of earth is filled with the lust of the flesh, the lust of the eyes and the pride of life.

3. Glory is the realm of all spiritual blessing.

4. The Ark of the Covenant is the most powerful type of His Glory in the Old Testament.

5. We must move from the place of grace to the place of Glory.

6. The Holy of Holies was the place where the focus was God and God alone.

Lucifer knows of the Glory of God and will try to prevent you from receiving.

Chapter 3

Changed by Glory!!

2 Cor. 3:17, 18 says, *"Now the Lord is that Spirit: and where the Spirit of the Lord is, there is liberty.*

18. But we all with open face beholding as in a glass the glory of the Lord, are changed into the same image from glory to glory, even as by the Spirit of the Lord."

These verses are immensely significant and are filled with Heavenly revelation in relation to a supernatural transformation. It begins by stating that, "...the Lord is that Spirit and where the Spirit of the Lord is there is liberty." One of the translations of this verse is amazingly relevant. It states: "Now the Lord is that Spirit and where the Spirit is Lord, there is free access." Where the presence of the Spirit is welcomed, encouraged and cherished, where the claims of the Spirit are unrivalled, there is free access.

The question of worship is of vital importance to access Glory. There are so many things that subtly upstage the claims of the Holy Spirit, the claims of Almighty God and the claims of Jesus on your life. Be it the dispensing of your time on private kingdom-building; be it the entanglements of life that have squeezed out of you, the commitment to God that should be freely given; be it the dreams that you have that have nothing to do with God and His kingdom; be it relationships that do not glorify God and lead you down the path of least resistance; be it the drive to survive to the extent that life is influenced by the unfettered desire to possess things. Anything that comes between you and God and His purposes for your life, soon becomes idolatrous if they are not dealt with. The devil will do all that he can to obstruct you and hinder you from getting to this Glory. This Glory is offered by God and the devil has no power to abort this offer. His avowed purpose is to introduce any temptation, any weakness, any alternative that will cause you to deviate or deter or detour from the path to Glory. He will do all that he can to deny you access to Glory. Divided allegiances, personal agendas, double-mindedness are all tools in the devil's workshop. God will not allow people to flow with or live in the dimension of Glory when their priority is fleshy, selfish and earthy.

THE QUESTION OF LORDSHIP

There comes the necessary question. How does the Spirit become Lord? It is within your power to make Him Lord of your life. The surrender of the will, so that it is not my will but His will be done, is the one thing that leads to Lordship as He begins to control the only thing that you have control over, your will. The only thing that hinders the will of God in your life is the will of man, your very own will. It is either your will or His will. You will never be able to have both at the same time.

Think about the meaning of this verse.

Matthew 6: 10 says, *"Thy will be done."*

The kingdom of God is that amazingly vast supernatural increase of God. In this kingdom, the Glory of God is the atmosphere. When the will of God is done, the kingdom of God comes into being and where the kingdom of God is in existence, the King executes His authority. In this realm, no force has the ability to countermand the dictates of the King. This is a time of unhindered execution. When God's kingdom comes, God's dimension is instituted and God's atmosphere flows, spiritual life ascends to its highest level. This is where we want to live, to flow, to breathe. This is life sublime, Heaven on earth, life to its fullest and eternity in the heart. All of this done, because the will of man has bowed to the will of God.

God has placed great emphasis on the free moral agency of man and the ability of man to make his own decisions apart from divine compulsion. It is within your power to submit your will to the will of the Lord or not. Never are you freer, though, or more liberated than when you live in this submission to His will. If you do what you can, God will do what you can't. God will never do the possible. You cannot change your heart and God won't change your mind but if you change your mind, God will change your heart. All of this is depending on our response to the will.

The middle letter of "sin" is I; the prominent letter in "liar" is I the middle letter in "pride" is I and the difference between "better" and "bitter" is I." "I" is at the centre of "sin, liar, pride" and "bitter." This "I", this self will, this intransigent letter, this perpendicular pronoun is at the centre of all evil, all flesh, all decay, all defeat, all discouragement and all distraction. To cherish and embrace this self will is a reflection of the depraved mind of man. It is this flesh, this self will, this absorption with "I" that has engineered the doom of so many lives. The path of life is strewn with the wreckage of lives that made self will their choice. The choice is elementary for the true believer: not my will but Thine be done.

FREE ACCESS

When the Holy Spirit is given control over your life, when your will is submitted to His will and His Lordship is established, there is now free access. In this moment, there is nothing that can stop you from having access. No past sin, no past failure, no power of the enemy, no attack of Satan. You have now been granted free access; the price has already been paid so access is free. The bondages of the enemy have been loosed so you are free: free in two dimensions. On the one hand, the price is paid so this is free; on the other hand, the bondage has been broken so I am free. When Jesus shed His blood, the work was done and finished. There is now no payment for this completed work. And now bondage by and to the enemy is broken, so I experience freedom from the power of the enemy. I have been unfettered. The veil has been torn down; the wall of hindrance has been removed so there is unrestricted access.

So many times the force of the enemy, memories from the past nurture failure, block entrance into fullness of life. Here in this time, when the Holy Spirit is Lord, I have access which means that nothing can stop me. That self will that bound me so I had no spiritual freedom, that will that stopped me and prohibited me from entering into the fullness of God's plan for my life, is now bound. I am free to become whatever God has ordained me to become and I have access to His fullness for my life.

Of course, the next question is, "Access to what?" This will be answered in a little while.

BUT WE ALL WITH OPEN FACE

The words, "We all...," break down distinctions. It does not matter what title you hold, what position you occupy or what stratum of society you live in. This involves you. So many times people live in self deluded worlds, with illusions of godhood, feeling that a different standard must or should apply to them. In this body of Christ, there is no bond or free, no Jew or Gentile, no rich no poor. Your elevated social or financial status has nothing to do with this matter of Gory. There is no different standard for those who consider themselves to be the "elite fleet."

The next words carry an entire dimension of revelation: **"...WITH OPEN FACE!"** This phrase means to uncover, to disclose, to unveil. The meaning extends to the fact that it is not a 1 hour or 1 day or 1 time unveiling. It must be a perpetual, daily, continuous unveiling. You must be willing to lift the thing that has covered you. You must be able to face the thing that tried to deface you. You cannot be so devastated by the past that you forget where you are now. You cannot be so enthralled by the future that you don't know the condition that you are in now. Before you get to the place that God wants you to be, there must be an honest assessment of where you are and who you are. You must be able to look in the mirror and face the reflection there. This ability to face the issue, this desire to recognise who you are, this determination to not avoid or escape is a necessary prerequisite for experiencing what God has in store.

Consider David for a moment. He was a liar, a manipulator, a murderer along with a few other undesirable qualities. Yet, despite all of this, God said, "He is a man after My heart." David's failure was obvious, his mismanagement was evident, his abuse of power was undeniable. How could God make such a statement? Psalm 51:3; 32:5 and 51:9 draw attention to David's heart. Here is the statement that touched the heart of God. "I will confess, I will acknowledge, I will not hide..." My sin is evident Father, I confess; my mistakes are many, I will acknowledge; my responsibility for my actions is here; I will not hide.

"I confess," means that I blame no one for my action. I have sinned and I confess that to you. I take responsibility for my actions because no one made me do what I did, so "I acknowledge." Shame is before me but I will not crawl into a corner of escape. Lord I will not hide. Here is the King of Israel facing himself and recognizing what he did and who he was. You must be able to see who you are and approach this with all honesty. If we face these issues, then Almighty God is ready to bring transformation in a way we never experienced. Whatever has to be removed, whatever veil, whatever veneer, whatever deception, let it be removed today. If we do not confess, if we do not acknowledge, if we do not declare, "I will not hide!" then we will never advance to where God wants us. All these things are within our power to do! To recognise! To remove! To rescind! To ask God to do what I can is to live in frustration. So I take responsibility.

A change is coming in this climate. Before the change comes, the veil must be removed according to II Cor.3: 17, 18. Whatever you are hiding behind must be removed. The danger of the flesh is that part of its operations is internal and invisible. Many find a place of comfort and ease in hiding behind the invisible because no one else around may know our issues. So we choose to be defined by the impressions that people have of us, not the content of our characters. We are more concerned with the label than the content so we live in a veil-covered life. I reiterate - that veil must be removed. We must come before the Lord with open face, with nothing to hide. It cannot be hidden from Him anyway so the attempt to hide is a part of the deception web that has been woven.

These are all the points that must be considered before we enter into Glory.

CHAPTER 3

Summary

1. Glory, by its very nature, brings dramatic change.

2. The Lordship of the Holy Spirit is the entrance to seeing God's demonstrations.

3. The submission of the will to God precedes the entrance of His Glory.

4. We all must come before Him with a perpetual unveiling of our lives.

5. We must be able to face who we are before we can become what we can be.

I will confess, I will acknowledge and I will not hide are the elements that open our lives.

Chapter 4

The Peril of Undue Familiarity

To think that Almighty God has bypassed the most ornate temples, the most embellished palaces and the most architecturally magnificent pyramids and made your body His temple, is amazing. He made you the house of His Glory. This is one of the most sobering thought-provoking facts in relation to God's love for you. Here you are, now, with all the potential for supernatural infusion, with the open door to live a Kingdom-oriented life in the midst of all the negatives of an oppressed world. This morning I am in New York City ready to go to speak, then I leave for Israel tomorrow and I feel totally overwhelmed by His Presence. After preaching for 39 years and travelling the world, the revelation has become more substantive than ever. I am His Temple. He has called and chosen me. His fire burns in my bosom. His Glory is in my life. I can't wait to see what will happen this morning as Heaven's dimension touches people.

So many Christians have become so familiar with divine things that they find it easy to live substandard lives. They have no desire to experience the fullness of God.

Colossians 2:9 says, *"For in Him dwelleth all the fullness of the godhead bodily."*

This verse speaks of God's fullness in His body which is the open door to a life of victory and power. A great part of the church is living like the tribes of Gad and Manasseh that refused to go into the Promised Land because the place where they were was rich and lush. There was grass and water but they were called to enter into warfare to drive out the enemies so that God's people could enter into their inheritance. When they came to the Jordan, they saw the side that was rich and fertile, a place that would be good for their cattle. Their lives could be lived in ease and convenience. They decided to stay there. What a cheap sell out, what a denial of a victorious tomorrow, what a refusal of a supernatural inheritance.

SELLING THE FUTURE FOR THE PRESENT

They had a promised land before them filled with all the potential for an ever-increasing life of fullness. There would be battles but the promise of victory was given even before they entered into battle. Sadly, even after seeing the miracle of the Passover, the glory of the Exodus, the sustained supply in the wilderness, they still chose the other side of Jordan. This is the temptation that so many Christians have succumbed to. They delight in the feeling of no responsibility, they revel in the lack of the need for obedience! They gladly accept the thought of no serious battle and no command to drive out the enemies. They forfeit the glories that await them for the complacent immediate moment. In church today, there is little time for prayer and intercession. The worship time is precisely structured, the speaking time is timed almost to the minute and now sermonettes are producing Christianettes. We must be out by noon on Sunday to give people time for fellowship. We spend over 40 hours per week in the workplace in the world. This world is a spirit, a system and a place. Its influence is constantly bombarding our lives and endeavouring to enter our hearts and minds. Now in the presence of God where there is fullness and pleasure, we have timed these heavenly moments. We gaze at the watch and there is the uneasy shuffle as noon hour on Sunday approaches. If the time element is more important than basking in the presence of God, then something vital has been lost. What is commonly not seen though, is that these border-dwellers, the tribes of Gad and Manasseh were the first to be killed by the invading forces of the enemy. The ones at ease, the complacent ones, the ones who settled for the material things were the first to be wiped out when the battle began. They had no power to resist because they were right where the enemy wanted them – on the outskirts, on the periphery.

Think of this! Delivered from Egypt, miracles all around them in the wilderness, the promise of a glorious tomorrow and here they lay, in lonely graves on the other side. Ease and complacency may add momentarily to fleshly comfort as selfish inclinations are appeased. However in the time of battle, where commitment, diligence and dedication are required, these complacent ones fall in defeat.

CREATED AND CALLED FOR HIGHER PURPOSE

1Corinthians 3:16 says, *"Know ye not that ye are the temple of God, and that the Spirit of God dwelleth in you?"*

This says that I am a temple created by God for supernatural function and supernatural destiny. Just as Jesus was God's Divine connection between Heaven and Earth while He was on earth, so too you are created to be like Jesus, housing the same presence. His physical body left the earth at the Ascension but it was only in preparation for a spiritual body on the day of Pentecost called the church. The body of Christ is the creation of God, to execute the purposes of God and to be His kingdom on earth. In this body, the reign of God will bring the execution of the authority of God. Here the Glory of God will bring the exhibition of God's kingdom. Just as the Old Testament Tabernacle was the place where the Glory was seen, so too in this body, the body of Christ, His Glory must be seen. Just as in the Temple, the Glory of God fell in the Holy of Holies, so too in this temple, the body of Christ, there must be the presence of His Glory. Is there any calling, any purpose, any destiny that is higher and more profound than this? **NO! 1000 times NO!!**

Yet in the midst of this Divine descent, this supernatural infusion, this Heavenly Glory, many have chosen a life of convenience and ease and have embraced a life of fleshly indulgence and worldly consumption. What will it take for the people sitting in the pew to realize that their God-given destiny is to house and function in His Heavenly touch, His Glory? The attraction of the present, the addiction to apathy are anathema to the greatness that the Lord has in store for you.

CONSIDER TWO TYPES OF TEMPLES.

Scripture speaks of 2 types of temples: one made of stone which was built in Israel; the other made of people touched by Almighty God: the church. When we begin to discuss the purpose of these temples, we must accept that the future of our lives must be driven by God's purpose. If you are created with God's purpose and you choose to live in a purpose framed by flesh and selfishness, life will become a mass of confusion.

In understanding where the Old Testament Temple would be built we must consider,

Genesis 22: 4-5 which states, *"Then on the third day Abraham lifted up his eyes and saw the place afar off*
5. And Abraham said unto his young men, Abide ye here with the ass; and I and the lad will go yonder and worship."

Abraham was given a son of promise whose name was Issac which means "laughter" and so, in accordance with his name, he brought his father much happiness. Abraham had a very special connection with Issac because he was the son of promise and the son of his old age. He was the miracle son that he had awaited for a long time. Here on Mt. Moriah, the Temple would be built and the first act performed on this mountain was an act of selflessness and an act of worship. Abraham was asked to surrender Issac to God. There are times when you have to surrender what you love the most to get what you need the most. In God's mind, though, the son would never be killed on the altar. Abraham, not knowing this, freely offered his son in obedience, surrender and utter abandonment to God.

Remember, this is the site on which the future temple would be built and this is where many are trapped and entangled. God demands surrender and obedience and there are many that are unwilling to surrender personal dreams, ambitions and wants. Issac was the repository of all Abraham's dreams, ambitions, desires, his future, the future of the world... according to Abraham's feelings and thought patterns. BUT Remember this! Almighty God would save Issac and when Issac returned, his name would be included in one of the appellations of God. He is known as the God of Abraham, Issac and Jacob. What God gives back is infinitely more than what is given to Him. The reason the enemy fights the believer so much in the area of surrender is that he knows that what is surrendered to God will have Heavenly multiplication. What is kept to self is divided, experiences subtraction but what is given to God experiences multiplication and addition. God is not asking you to surrender what is best for you to take what is best for Himself. His heart, His purpose is to give you Heaven's best but this cannot be given without your surrender.

One of the meanings of the word Moriah is "the fear of God." It means reverence for God that demands the obedience, respect and the adoration of the One who comes to this mountain. I find it amazing that God would build His Temple here in the future and the first noted act on this mountain, was Abraham's surrender of the one he loved dearly. This would become the foundational principle, the pivotal point, the absolute indispensable prerequisite for building the Temple to house God's Glory. Death to the flesh is seen as Abraham offered his greatest love, Issac. He laid all his aspirations on this altar that was built with his own hands. This must be a powerful, personal lesson for you and your future. The Temple can only be built, the Glory will only come when we are willing to be obedient, in surrender, when we are willing to build the altar with our own hands. To hold fast to the things that you cherish, to grasp the things that you love, only means that you have forfeited this mighty building of God in you.

What is given in surrender is returned in Glory. It is within your power to make that surrender a reality right now. It is within your reach, your capability to make this decision and see the descent of the Glory of God. I will not be dominated by the dominion of darkness. I will not be ruled by the tyranny of self controlling me.

TODAY I SURRENDER! TODAY I AM OBEDIENT!

THE SECOND PRINCIPLE

I Chronicles 21: 22 -24 states, *"Then David said to Ornan, Grant me the place of this threshing floor, that I may build an altar therein unto the Lord; thou shalt grant it me for the full price: that the plague may be stayed from the people.*

23. And Ornan said unto David, Take it to thee, and let my lord the king do that which is good in his eyes: lo I give thee the oxen also for burnt offerings, and the threshing instruments for the wood and the wheat for the meat offering; I give it all.

24. And King David said to Ornan, Nay; but I will verily buy it for the full price: for I will not take that which is thine for the lord, nor offer burnt offerings without cost."

David was a man that was supernaturally chosen to be king. Even before he was king, his life was a sequence of divine interventions as he valiantly slew the lion and the bear. However the king fell into the trap of flesh and committed terrible sins before the Lord. But the king was now to build an altar on Ornan's threshing floor. The place where this threshing floor was located was Mt. Moriah, the same place that Abraham offered Issac to God. David was offered this spot without cost but he refused to offer to Almighty God, what cost him nothing. What a testimony of the heart of this king. This is an area where so many are tempted. They are tempted to give to God what cost them nothing. So many today are looking for their own way to God, their own way of worship, their own way of surrender. Instead of changing their lives to conform to the Word, they endeavour to change the Word to conform to their lives. In doing this, they are trying to create their own Christ. Their lives become crossless and costless. I will not offer to God that which costs me nothing. Fleshly control, fleshly dictates will not rule my life where I look for the shortcut. Whatever price I have to pay to give my all to God, with willingness and joy, I pay this price.

There is another profound thought in these verses. Ornan was a Jebusite and by birth was heathen. However by choice, he was a convert. The Jebusites were doomed for their iniquities and at one time, they had captured Jerusalem. Yet the Temple would be built on the threshing floor of a heathen who was converted. The word Ornan means, "He who bows." Here, the religious bigotry of the heathen, the pride and arrogance of false religion had to bow. The Temple would be built on the property of a Jebsuite who was a heathen. Your past can be nullified because of your desire to bow to the Lord God Almighty.

These two points are vitally connected to God's building. They are illustrative of the greatest hindrances to the building of God's Temple where His Glory falls. With Abraham it is the principle of surrendering that which is loved; with David, it is refusing to offer to God that which cost him nothing. The two greatest struggles in the lives of God's people are at the point of surrender and obedience and the temptation to live a costless life. Sadly it is what often interferes with this God-designed process of building His temple in the believer.

We must never become so unduly familiar with Divine things that we lose the sense of awe at His Presence and Glory. We must never take for granted this supernatural purpose for which we are saved by displaying a convenient commitment to God. We are saved to serve, we are saved to be worshippers, we are called unto His purpose. This purpose must be realized and followed. I will worship Him, I will serve Him, I will follow His purpose Cherished indulgences, embraced habits, protected possessions must never, never, never, never rob us of the Glory that God has for us.

CHAPTER 4

Summary

1. We must guard our hearts so that we do not become unduly familiar with Divine things.

2. Your body has become a temple to house His Glory.

3. Many sell their future for a fleshly present.

4. There is a responsibility that must be accepted if the privilege is to be enjoyed.

5. You are called for His higher purpose.

6. Be willing to give up what you love to get what you need to be obedient to God.

The attempt is to make your life costless and crossless and this must change.

Chapter 5

The Glory–The Temple– The Throne

Isaiah 6: 1-6 states, *"In the year that King Uzziah died I saw also the Lord sitting upon a throne, high and lifted up, and his train filled the temple.*

2. Above it stood the seraphims: each one had six wings; with twain he covered his face, and with twain he covered his feet, and with twain he did fly.

3. And one cried unto another, and said, Holy, holy, holy is the Lord of Hosts: the whole earth is full of his glory.

4. And the posts of the door moved at the voice of him that cried, and the house was filled with smoke.

5. Then said I, Woe is me! For I am a man of unclean lips and I dwell in the midst of a people of unclean lips: for mine eyes have seen the King, the Lord of hosts.

6. Then flew one of the seraphims unto me, having a live coal in his hand, which he had taken with the tongs from off the altar: And he laid it upon my mouth, and said, Lo, this hath touched thy lips and thine iniquity is taken away and thy sin purged."

This is a unique insight into the throne room in Heaven and some of the activities that surround the throne of God. We see the Lord sitting upon the throne with His Glory all around and the seraphim surround the throne. We hear the words of the seraphim in relation to the throne and we see the atmosphere in the throne room. We see as well the effect of the throne-room atmosphere on Isaiah's life. We see the presence of fire, its cleansing effect on Isaiah, and his commission to go. But in this text in verse 1, the first few words show the reality of the existence of two kings: King Uzziah and the Lord of Hosts. In every life, there is the presence of two kings that are contending for rulership in that life. King Uzziah represents human, reign and the Lord of Hosts demonstrates the reign of Almighty God in your life. All of life's issues emanate from the rulership of King Uzziah or the Lord of Hosts in your life. The quality of your life or the lack thereof, is a consequence of rulership. The question of ruling and reigning becomes therefore, the most powerful issue of the internal life. It is an issue that is only decided by you because you are the only one, through the power of your free will, who occupies the seat of authority in your life. The matter of occupation cannot be relegated or put upon someone else. No external force, no family connection, no voice that is around you has the power to choose which king is in control of your life. This is a deeply personal choice that is firmly placed within the realm of your personal control.

There are so many times that Christians blame the circumstances, the relationship with others, the surrounding trials, for the decisions they make. No one has the power to make you choose. This is your God-given right and responsibility - so you choose this day whom you will serve. Personal responsibility must be accepted. It is the age old record from the book of Genesis when temptation provides a suggestion but the act of eating is made through personal choice.

KING UZZIAH

The magnitude of the revelation of verse 1 is absolutely amazing. There is a strange paradox in the life of Uzziah that reflects in the first words of the text: "In the year that King Uzziah died..." The name Uzziah means "the strength of God" and this was seen in the many accomplishments of Uzziah. He ascended the throne at the young age of sixteen. And he engaged in some military campaigns with significant success. He battled with the Philistines, the Amorites and others. And he also had great success in agricultural exploits. He dug wells and built towers and increased the land's productivity. He also diverted time and attention to building an army and so naturally, because of his accomplishments, great attention was focussed on the king. Great hopes and aspirations were placed in him and his reign.

But, all, the parade and pageantry, the great accomplishments of the king came to an abrupt end. He was stricken with leprosy. This was God's punishment upon him. How could a king with so much potential and good works, come, under Divine judgement? Here is the answer: the king chose to blatantly violate the Law, to contravene the Word of God and usurp the place of the priest. He stole the priest's function. So great was his success, so adoring his subjects, so applauded and approved was he, that he felt it right to break the Law. The King's role was to execute authority in the land but the function in the Temple was strictly given to the priests. To offer a sacrifice in rebellion and violation of this, was to incur the wrath of the Almighty. Uzziah was, therefore, stricken with leprosy. He degenerated from "the strength of God" to the strength of a man because of one lethal, evil choice – the choice to be his own law, to violate God's law and to occupy a position that was never his.

This is a judgement, an indictment, a punishment that must reverberate and resonate in our lives. No matter how great the accomplishment, how great the approval or how loud the applause, we do not have the right to violate the law of God and break the commands of God. So many have been spiritually numbed by success that they have lost their sensitivity to God and their devotion to Him because of these very

accomplishments and successes. Spiritual senses are numbed as a result, dedication is diverted and allegiance to God now has a rival - the flesh. Fleshly ambition has taken the place of Godly commitment. Think about this for a moment. This is one of the two things that want to occupy the seat of authority in your life. If this "Flesh-king" takes this position in your life, think of what this occupation will reproduce in you. Selfish rule, selfish ambition, the violation of God's law and defilement in the Temple. How many people are offering sacrifices or functioning in the Temple and are doing so in rebellion and violation? If there is to be an experience in the Throne Room, if you are to be touched by His Glory, if you are to see a revelation of the Lord, King Uzziah must die. There will be no revelation of Heaven and no descent of Glory if your life is ruled by the king of rebellion and flesh. A king called and touched by God, successful and powerful, can fall into a trap, feeling that he has the right to violate God's law and so descend into a leprous judgement.

THE KING – HIGH AND LIFTED UP!

When Uzziah died, Isaiah saw the Lord. Vision of the Lord is impaired by focus on the wrong king so there must be a death before there is entry into another dimension. Your heart is a throne and the enemy will constantly endeavour to install godless things to rule on this throne of your heart. These things must die because the outcome of your life will be decided by who occupies the throne of your life. This Uzziah, this king, these ruling influences must die. This death is not a weekly or monthly ritual. It has to be a daily death. The enemy tries on every corner, seizes every opportunity to bring your life under the subjection of a godless rule. We must deal with these attacks of the enemy on a daily basis.

Here is the Lord, high and lifted up with His train filling the Temple. Here is Uzziah on a throne and he must die.

Paul said in Romans 6:12, *"Let not sin therefore reign in your mortal body..."*

Sin has not come just to sit and maintain; it has come to be king and to reign, it has come to establish rulership. The words "Let not," means that it is within your power to prohibit or permit. It is within your power to terminate the rulership of this king.

When Uzziah died, Isaiah had a life-changing vision. He saw the Lord sitting upon the throne. There was a superior, Heavenly Presence in the throne room and it was the Lord sitting on the Throne of Heaven. This means many things. The implication of the Lord sitting upon the throne contains a vast realm of revelation. It means that He occupies the place of authority in Heaven. It means that there is none that is able to rival Him. It means above Him there is no other. It means that no force, power, people or cartel can remove Him. When Isaiah saw the Lord, this is whom he saw. This vision would empower him, energize him and absorb him. With this on his heart, no obstacle would be prohibitive, no external power or circumstance would stop him.

The vision would be his momentum for the rest of his life. He saw the Lord High and lifted up and His train filled the Temple. The train was that flowing part of the regal garments of the King that would be draped around the Throne. That train would surround the Throne and be illustrative of the magnificence of the king. In Isaiah 6, the train was the Glory of the Lord that filled the throne room.

In Revelation Chapters 4 and 5, there is a peek into the Throne Room and a view of the Presence of Glory.

Revelation 21:23 states, *"And the city had no need of the sun, neither of the moon, to shine in it: for the glory of God did lighten it, and the Lamb is the Light thereof."*

Here in Heaven, the Glory of the Lord lit up the city. What a glorious plan Almighty God had for Isaiah but for a while, his vision seemed to be blocked. What is blocking your vision today? Why have not more people seen this Glory? What earthly power has stopped this Heavenly vision? What hinders you from experiencing this Throne Room Glory? The devil will do all he can to hinder you, to blur your vision, to stop you from seeing the Lord high and lifted up. He knows that from the moment you receive this vision, from the moment King Uzziah dies, your life will never be the same. His only power is to tempt you to be consumed by the earthly, the worldly, so that you never see and work in the power of the Heavenly. Lucifer knew the Glory, the Presence, the power of the Heavenly. He has first hand knowledge of this Heavenly potential so he will do all he can to stop this from becoming your substance, your inheritance.

If you let the earthly things the world courts, if you allow the things of this world, or King Uzziah who represents the rival kingdom of this world. to rule you, you have robbed yourself of a bit of Heaven on earth. In God's realm, His Glory fills that Temple. In your realm, Almighty wants that Glory to fill your life. This filling of Glory will be the consequence of His occupation of your life, your throne, your heart.

Think about this for a moment. Lucifer knew the power of the atmosphere of Heaven. He was kicked out for trying to violate that atmosphere. He brought to earth the atmosphere of rebellion and violation and this is what he endeavours to reproduce in the lives of people here. He knows that when the atmosphere of Heaven enters a life, there is no power, force or situation that can stand in its way. So he raises Uzziahs, he erects flesh-barriers; he emphasizes the earthly and the worldly. Many gullible people have sold out their lives for momentary gratification. The temptation to ease, complacency and apathy have won their vote. What a subtle web the enemy has spun to bind the lives of many to spiritual weakness and poverty.

What today fills your temple? What surrounds your heart? A choice must be made; neutrality is not an option. Choose your king and choose him now! Is your choice going to be Uzziah, rebellion and violation and addiction to earthiness? Or is your choice going to be the Lord, High and Lifted Up with His train filling the Temple? You face a major decision that will have a direct bearing on the life you live and the potential of your future. Choose Uzziah and have rebellion, violation and degeneration rule and reign in you. Or choose the Lord and have His Presence and Glory fill your life. Have a vision that will never lose its potency. I have been asked by many, "How can you humanly maintain this schedule, the intensity of the vision after 39 years of ministry?" My answer is that this has nothing to do with humanity but everything to do with divinity. It is because of Almighty God and His abiding Presence, His fire and His Glory. This has nothing to do with earthly approval but with Heavenly connection. After 39 years of preaching, I feel more power, more focus, more infusion than ever before. I hope you can sense this in my writing because it is my fervent desire to be more and do more for My Master.

Make your decision and live with the results. It is a wonderful moment when you see the Lord High and Lifted Up, to see His train filling the Temple and to receive a vision and a Heavenly infusion that will give you momentum for the rest of your life.

THE THRONE AND THE TEMPLE

We are still in verse 1 of Isaiah 6. This verse presents the revelation of the Throne and the Temple. The Throne sits above the Temple. From the Temple comes worship and from the Throne come authority and Glory and this Glory fills the Temple. It is very important to understand the function of the Temple and the Throne. The Temple is created to house the Glory of God. This was the case in the Old Testament; it will be the case in the New Testament; it will be the case in the New Jerusalem it is the case today in your life. Yes, you are the temple of the Lord created to house His Presence. From this temple comes worship. There is no descent of Glory, there is no reception of Glory, there is no life of Glory without worship. In the Old Testament, it was on Yom Kippur, the Day of Atonement when a sacrifice was made that the Glory of God filled the Temple. When the Temple was dedicated, after sacrifices were offered, the Glory of God filled the Temple. Please note that you were made a temple to offer sacrifices of praise, joy and thanksgiving. Yes, in your worship, you find your truest function. As I travel around the world, in most churches, you have to solicit the praise of the people for God, you have to ask them to worship and after 15 or 30 seconds, they are finished. There is little intensity, little effort, little determination to be true worshippers. So many are led by the circumstance, by the surroundings, by the pressured feeling of the moment. So many are entangled with the affairs of life that they forget what their life is about.

1Peter 2:9 says, *"But ye are a chosen generation, a royal priesthood, an holy nation, a peculiar people, that ye should shew forth the praise of Him who hath called you out of darkness into His marvellous light."*

It says that you are a chosen generation, a royal priesthood, a holy nation, a peculiar people so that you should do something. You are this so that you will do this. What should you do? You should show forth the praises of Him who has called you out of the darkness into His marvellous light. Have you been called? Are you called out of darkness? Are you called into his marvellous light? Yes on all counts. Now you are to show forth His praises. So if you are this, and you should be doing this, then not doing it negates your reason for being. You are to show forth His praises, not because the circumstance is great, or the feeling is right or everything is in order. No I show forth His praises because this is why I am a chosen generation, a royal priesthood, a holy nation, a peculiar people. Many have negotiated themselves into weakness, defeat and irrelevance. You are a temple so you must worship. This is the purpose of the temple. END OF STORY! When the worship comes from this temple, it touches the Throne room of God. Let nothing and no one, no circumstance, no trial or trauma stop you from your right to worship. You belong to the victorious assembly of the chosen ones. Let the redeemed of the Lord say so! We are victors not victims. We are worshippers not whiners. The Throne is engaged when the temple is functioning as it was designed to. Now here comes the execution of authority and the descent of Glory.

In everything that God does, there is order. That is why Gethsemane comes before Calvary, Calvary before the grave, the grave before resurrection, resurrection before ascension and ascension before Pentecost. So many people want the more of God without the order of God. If there is no worship, or God's order, there will be no Heavenly vision and no life of Glory. It was when Uzziah died that Isaiah saw the Lord and the Glory sequence ensued. You cannot be so fleshly bound that you refuse to be a worshipper and continue to expect the Glory of a Heavenly descent. Something must leave earth before something leaves Heaven. There is a personal responsibility that must be assumed before you can receive the privilege of a Heavenly descent.

CHAPTER 5

Summary

1. The throne in Heaven and my temple on earth are vitally connected.
2. King Uzziah had to be removed from the throne to allow the vision of the King of Kings.
3. When there is worship in the temple, there is a descent of Glory from the throne.
4. Satan knows of Glory so he will do all that he can to hinder you from living in it.
5. Two kings are striving for your allegiance and one must be chosen.

Something must leave earth for something to leave Heaven.

Chapter 6

THE THRONE:
The Temple; The Glory–Part II

Now that we are engaged in this Heavenly vision, we observe the actions of the seraphim. Each one had six wings, and with two they covered their face, with two their feet, with two, they did fly. It is interesting that the first thing that they do is to cover their face. This means that in the Presence of God, only the face of God must be seen: the face of man must be hidden. This is one of the major problems in church life where there are many who feel that their faces must be seen. The problem lies in the showiness of the face. May I humbly state that God was alive before you came and He will be alive long after you are gone. May I state that the body of Christ was alive and thriving before your talent appeared. May I suggest that there was salvation and success before your vote. May I state that God is God all by Himself. You must consider being a servant of God as your highest honour. All the glory and honour must go to Our Lord who has called us and any attempt to subvert that honour is a gross sin. Would to God that the attitude of our people would be the eradication of personal showiness and instead there would be the complete emphasis on the face of God. Lucifer's great sin in Isaiah 14 was that he wanted to be the light, not the reflection. The enemy of our souls tries to reproduce this attitude in the lives of God's people, so that they too will be banished from God's realm.

Isaiah 14: 12-15 says, *"How art thou fallen from Heaven, O Lucifer, son of the morning! How art thou cut down to the ground, which didst weaken the nations!*

13. For thou hast said in thine heart, I will ascend into Heaven, I will exalt my throne above the stars of God: I will sit also upon the mount of the congregation, in the sides of the north:

14. I will ascend above the heights of the clouds; I will be like the Most High.

15. Yet thou shalt be brought down to hell, to the sides of the pit."

As you study these verses, you find the desire of Lucifer was summed up in 5 "I wills," that all had to do with his showiness. Because of this he was cast out of Heaven. Let all the honour and all the glory go to God and succumb to no temptation to take the credit for what God is doing. Be happy to be used of the Master as an instrument. Be happy to be called His servant. Use no talent or gift to draw attention to you.

With two wings, the seraphim covered their feet. This refers to the devotion to Almighty God. This is an element that surrounds the Throne of God. There must be devotion to Him and to Him alone. Today, devotion has been challenged so that lives have been divided and their focus diluted. Whatever commands your highest devotion, that is your god. So many have become devoted to things of little spiritual significance and their time is allotted to things that are of personal interest. There is no time for prayer, study, evangelism because life has become cluttered with a flurry of world-oriented activity. God does not hold you accountable for the hours spent on your job because this is your responsibility. He holds you accountable for the negotiable hours. Devotion decides how these hours are dispensed. It is incorrect to say that you have no time to pray, study or be involved in the work of God. It is correct to say that what we are devoted to decides the dispensing of our time.

Then with two wings, the seraphim did fly. This speaks of service. Remember we are talking about Throne-Room elements. Service comes from devotion and is an automatic response to devotion to

Our Lord. In devotion I bow, in service I walk. There are so many in church life that find service to be demanding and difficult. They are constantly overwhelmed by the demands of service. However, when you are devoted to the Lord, service is a spontaneous reaction because in every way, your desire is to please Him. I am not frustrated by service: I am honoured by the opportunity to be of service.

THE RESULTS OF GLORY:

The seraphim cried to each other, "Holy, Holy, Holy," is the Lord of Hosts. Here in the Throne-Room, they are crying to one another about the Holiness of God. This is something that needs to be reproduced in church life today. So many speak of so many things that are negative, critical and destructive to church life. I wonder what would happen in service on Sunday morning if people went around saying, "Holy, Holy, Holy is the Lord of Hosts." I believe atmospheres would be transformed by the power of this word. When the holiness of God is emphasized and verbalized, then all the other things must submit to this confession. The seraphim continued to say, "Holy, Holy, Holy is the Lord of Hosts."

Isaiah saw the Lord high and lifted up and the seraphim call Him the Lord of Hosts. I must ask a question. How do you see the Lord? Do you see Him above all with no limitation? He is seen by the angels as the Lord of Hosts which is the Old Testament designation for the commander in battle. He is not only Lord in the Throne-Room in Heaven, He is Lord over all that is in the earth. Isaiah saw Him high and lifted up and the seraphim saw Him as Lord of Hosts. In the presence of His Glory, in His Throne-Room, this is what you see. He wants to show you His absolute Lordship, His Glory and power, His willingness to fight on your behalf. How puny these little enemies look in the presence of such Lordship.

The third thing they said is, "The whole earth is full of His Glory." This must become substance to the child of God. So many testify of what is around them and negative words trap them in a prison of lack. When the angels looked from the Throne-Room, the whole earth was full of His Glory. Here are two perspectives of the same earth: the man who is bound sees the world as a prison; yet the angels say that the whole earth is full of His Glory. One is looking through the lens of earthiness and worldliness and saying how defeated, depressed and discouraging the world is. The other is saying from the Throne-Room looking through the lens of His Glory, "The whole earth is full of His Glory." He is in control and He will move in every situation. Think about these elements that are around the Throne that can become substance to you today

GLORY MOVES THE IMMOVEABLE

Verse 4 says, "...the post of the door moved at the voice of him that cried." When you open a door, the door frame or the posts of the door are generally not moved. The door moves but the doorposts do not. They are fixed and immoveable. In the Throne-Room of God, where His Glory is, whatever is immoveable is moved by the power and the Glory of God. Things that have been fixed in your lives and have not been able to be moved, when God's Glory comes, they are unfixed and moved by the power of God. Whatever has been stubbornly planted, whatever has been blocking you, today will be moved by the Glory of the Almighty. When God fills your life, the posts will be moved by the power of the Almighty. When God fills your life, the posts are moved by the power of God.

Then the house was filled with smoke which is the Old Testament symbol of the Glory of God. Now Isaiah speaks again. These are his first words after his encounter with Heaven. He says, "Woe is me, because I am a man of unclean lips and I dwell in the midst of a people of unclean lips, for my eyes have seen the King, the Lord of Hosts."

He did not say, "I am a prophet," or "I feel so filled," or "God has given me such gifts," or "I've seen angels." He saw His inner condition and his cry was, "Woe is me, I am a man of unclean lips..." Help me Lord, help my language. First help me then help how I speak. Some today, if they had had this experience, the first thing they would do is publicize it on every form of media. Isaiah's cry was, "Woe is me," help me deliver me. If only our people would have this encounter. So many are hung up on elaborate titles and if those titles are not given to them, it is near a crime against their reputation. How pathetic is this position! Isaiah, when he saw the Lord, saw Heavenly Glory and cried out, "Woe is me!"

Consider the three aspects of this vision. He saw the Lord which was the upward vision. He saw himself which was the inward vision. He saw others which was outward vision. He was then touched by the fire of God as the coal was laid upon his mouth. His lips were touched, his iniquity was taken away and sin purged. In the Presence of His Glory comes His Fire. Now Isaiah says, "Here am I, send me."

GLORY IN YOU TOUCHES
THE WORLD AROUND YOU

In John 17:23, the Scripture says, "... and that the world may know that thou has sent me, and hast loved them, as thou hast loved me." When the Glory of God is mentioned here, God speaks of the world. "That the world may know," is the heart of God. It is the heart of God to fill us with His Glory so that the world may know. Here in Isaiah 6 after the Heavenly encounter with Glory, holiness and fire, Isaiah says, "Lord, here I am send me." When you see the Lord, when the heavens are opened and you are touched by His Glory, you see yourself, then others. So many times it is easy to find fault with others, to emphasize their flaws and failures, but Isaiah saw himself. After this he saw others and his response was for the Lord to send him. He was there, present, ready and accounted for.

Let not your Heavenly encounter end with an emotional stirring that is but for a moment. Let not this moment when Heaven and earth become one, be just a "goose-bump" experience. Rather, let it be life-transforming and let it launch you into service for the Master like you have never seen. Note though, that service is not what comes first. This service is born out of devotion and reverence. "Here am I send me," are the last words in verse 8. It was the final summation after what had transpired. We ask, "Why is there not more of this in the church? Where are those who will say, 'Send me!'" We desperately need this opening of Heaven, this touch of Glory, this Holy Fire to be upon our lives. May we be able to say, "Here am I, send me."

CHAPTER 6

Summary

1. The seraphim cover their faces in the presence of God.

2. Personal showiness in the church must be eradicated.

3. The seraphim cry, "Holy, Holy, Holy..." and they see the Lord, high and lifted up.

4. How do you see the Lord?

5. In Heaven, the posts were moved by Glory. In your lives, the immoveable is moved by Glory.

6. Isaiah saw himself after he saw God's Glory.

The end result of this Glory was – "Here I am send me."

Chapter 7

DON'T ASK GLORY TO RETURN
If you don't know why Glory left

In the Old Testament, the most outstanding symbol of the Presence of God was the Ark of the Covenant. It was the heart of God, the Throne of God, the reign of God among His people. The Glory only fell when the Ark was present. As long as the Ark was in the possession of God's people, no enemy, no matter how powerful, was able to conquer or defeat the nation of Israel. With that Ark, they were invincible. It was the most precious thing in the entire nation. In I Samuel 4, tragedy struck the nation of Israel and the unthinkable, the unspeakable happened. Philistines defeated the nation of Israel and the sons of Eli were killed, the Ark was stolen and taken away by these enemies. When the messenger came to the Temple to tell the High Priest Eli of this, he first delivered the news of Eli's sons who had been killed. Then he told Eli that the Ark had been taken. When Eli heard that the Ark was gone, he fell backward and broke his neck. The suggestion is that the news of the death of his sons was painful but the news that the Ark was taken from Israel was unbearable. He could not live without the presence of God. Eli had filled the unique position of having been priest and judge of Israel for 40 years. As High Priest, he was vitally connected to the Ark on Yom Kippur, the Day of Atonement. So he knew that nothing, no death, no loss, no defeat could have more lethal and devastating results to the entire life of the nation than the loss of the Ark of the Covenant.

When God first gave the instruction to build the sanctuary, it was so that He could dwell among the people. The sanctuary was also called the Holy Temple of God, the Tent of Communion, the Sanctuary of God, the Sanctuary of the Testimony. All of these indicated the heart of God to dwell among His people, to place His Glory in their hearts. His Divine Presence would be in the tabernacle and this presence called "Shekinah" would rest on the Ark. God, furthermore, instructed that the Ark be built before anything else related to the Tabernacle because of its importance to worship for the nation of Israel.

THE MERCY SEAT AND CONTENTS OF THE ARK

Whereas the general body of the Ark was gold and wood, the mercy seat was made of pure gold. Gold and wood symbolize the divinity and humanity of Jesus. Jesus became the God-Man, fully God and fully man. The mercy seat, which formed the lid of the Ark, was to be made of pure gold and this mercy seat, this place where God met with this people, had to be untinged and untouched by the human element.

Now, within the Ark, there were three things of vital importance to the nation of Israel: the tablets of the Law, the pot of manna and the rod of Aaron. Each of these had enormous symbolic significance to the nation of Israel and to an understanding of the future of the nation. The Law would represent Jesus as my only law, my rule. The pot of manna would represent Jesus as the bread of life. The budding rod of Aaron would represent Jesus as my life. Remember it was this dead rod of Aaron that budded fruit overnight that authenticated Aaron's priesthood. So too Jesus, from the death of the cross, budded into life and resurrection, authenticating all His claims as the Son of God, the Saviour. There is no way in this book that I could give adequate treatment to the Ark of the Covenant. But you must know that this Ark, in the sanctuary, in the Temple was the absolute centre of the life of the nation of Israel.

What could lead to the loss of the Ark? What sin, failure, rebellion or violation could be so serious that it would lead to this? Why would this Divine

Presence depart? I will now proceed to give an explanation.

THE DANGER OF CLOSENESS

I Samuel 2: 12-17 states, *"Now the sons of Eli were sons of Belial; they knew not the Lord.*

13 And the priests' custom with the people was, that, when any man offered sacrifice, the priest's servant came, while the flesh was in seething, with a fleshhook of three teeth in his hand;

14 And he struck it into the pan, of kettle, or caldron, or pot; all that the fleshhook brought up the priest took for himself. So they did in Shiloh unto all the Israelites that came thither.

15. Also before they burnt the fat, the priest's servant came, and said to the man that sacrificed, Give flesh to roast for the priest; for he will not have sodden flesh of thee but raw.

16. And if any man said unto him, Let them not fail to burn the fat presently, and then take as much as thy soul desireth; then he would answer him, Nay; but thou shalt give it me now: and if not, I will take it by force.

17. Wherefore the sin of the young men was very great before the Lord: for men abhorred the offering of the Lord.

These verses begin with surprising and shocking words. The sons of Eli, the High Priest were sons of Belial. How could the sons of the High Priest, the sons of a judge be the sons of Belial? This would mean that they were wicked and worthless. Sons who knew about the covenant, knew about the priesthood and knew about the sanctuary. Sons that knew about the Ark and the Glory of God; sons that saw Divine manifestations and yet they were called wicked. Closeness does not mean likeness. So even though for all of their lives, they were in close proximity, they did not go to the next step to become like what they were close to. This is an area of immense danger and deception. It is the temptation to think that you have a reprieve, a different standard because you are genetically blessed. Their father was God's man and they were the devil's puppets. They had information, not transformation; they had it in the head not in their hearts; they had a profession not a possession.

This is a sobering cry to people today who sit in the house of God boasting of association but no transformation. Two thieves came close to Jesus, but they both had two different opinions, two different attitudes and two different destinies. They were both in close proximity but chose different directions. Do not be fooled by proximity for there are many that are close to the Ark but may die next to the Ark like Uzza and Ahio. Many have succumbed to the temptation of just enough, just enough to feel good, just enough to have a spasmodic experience, just enough to get by (barely), just enough to have a momentary blessing, just enough to feel marginally spiritual. To these people, there is no need for depth or determination, no need for consistency or character, no need for relevance or restoration. With the very little that they have, with the conveniently created lifestyle with accommodation and association, they have addicted themselves to the average. Yes I know they boast, "I am close to the Pastor, I am in church, I attend the socials, I even give when I can." In this text, the sons of the High Priest lived the lowly lives of wickedness and worthlessness. They were the most privileged; the most blessed; the most favored; but became the most cursed. The ballad of these is that, "It could have been different."

CLOSE BUT NOT COMMITTED

I was close but not committed, I was in it, but it was not in me. I had the Divine privilege but aborted it by not assuming my personal responsibility. My choice was the choice of appeasement, avarice and it led to my untimely death among enemies. When I could have been the victor, I became the victim. I wore a cloak of deception, I lived a life of ease, I refused my responsibilities and denied myself of the privilege. It was my doing. Others saw me with the external cloak and I may have been accepted and applauded but no one around me knew of the decay on the inside. I lived, I lost, I lied and then I died.

The name of one of the High Priest's sons, Hophni, means, "He who covers." This meaning accurately describes the way he lived. His life was a daily cover up where after every lie, every deception, he himself had to devise a strategy to cover his actions. Phinehas, the other son, had a name that means, "A bold countenance." This too became a reflection of his life as he arrogantly and boldly approached the things of God with a deeply selfish motive. There was no hesitation to commit the abominable no reluctance to claim for himself, what only belonged to God. Their end, their demise was at the point of the enemy's sword.

The record of these men's lives as documented in I Samuel 2:12 continues to spiral downward. It says, *"They knew not the Lord."* Some translations say, *"They regarded not the Lord,"* or, *"They loved not the*

Lord. " How could men of such stature, with such a heritage, with such divine blessing, "know not the Lord?" There is a difference between intellectual acceptance and heart commitment. The one has to do with a superficial, surface response. This response is not internal, there is no internal confession and it does not bring transformation on any level. It is totally on the informational, mental level. The Bible says that the demons believe and they tremble. This intellectual acceptance is totally superficial; the acceptance of a fact is where it begins and ends. When there is no change of heart, there is no change of life. When someone says that he believes, but it is not reflected in the quality of life that he lives, it is an indication that the belief is merely mental, intellectual and superficial. This is the satanic deception, the devilish duplicate. Give someone the thought that they have made a spiritual step when all they have done is stopped at the place of mental assent.

The saying, "It's all in the mind," becomes the reality of their life. We must strive with vigorous effort, never to be in this place.

The lives and deaths of Hophni and Phineas must be continuous reminders to us that superficial commitment and mental acceptance have nothing to do with heart transformation. Information mentally must lead to transformation internally. Mental acceptance requires no personal responsibility so the temptation to comfort and ease arises. Heart transformation, on the other hand, desires responsibility. I happily assume the responsibility of obedience, sacrifice and I joyfully pursue the call of God.

THE LETHAL REASON

What action would be so grave, what reason so lethal, that it would cause the loss of the Ark and the departure of the Glory of God? Even as I write this, my inner man shudders at the thought of the departure of the Glory of God. What could a person do, what position could he take, what act could have been perpetrated that would lead to such a thing? Words fail miserably in an attempt to describe the implications of the departure of the Glory of God.

It all had to do with the Temple, the sacrifice and the priests. It was the custom of the priests that when a sacrifice was offered, the servant of the priest would come when the flesh of the sacrifice was seething and plunge a flesh hook into the pan and whatever meat the flesh hook grabbed, would be taken for the priest. The fat of the animal sacrifice had to be burnt because the richest part of the sacrifice belonged to the Lord.

That which was ordained for God must be given to no other. But something went awry and the entire custom and sacrifice were violated by Hophni and Phineas. They demanded the meat, which was actually already theirs, but they also demanded that the portion which belonged to the Lord be given to them. They were interfering with the portion of the sacrifice that belonged to the Lord, demanding it for themselves. According to I Samuel 2: 12-17, they would take this by force if necessary. Not only did they dare to take what was meant for God, but they were willing to employ force to take this meat for themselves. They invoked a triple jeopardy upon their lives by their demanding behaviour. Demonic, demented, destructive, damnable only begin to explain the behaviour of these sons of the High Priest. The departure of God's Glory had to do with the attitude and actions of the sons of the High Priest. It had to do with the internal operations of the Temple and the acts of violation committed by the chosen.

God said of these men, that their sin was very great before the Lord for they abhorred the offering to the Lord. Their sin was before the Lord for it was an affront to His Word. By committing this act, they were showing contempt for the offering of the Lord. To come to the Temple with such action, to approach the sacrifice with such contempt, to violate the custom with such force would have to be the work of calloused, contemptuous, conniving men.

THE DOOM OF ELI

God called Eli, he chose Eli to be His priest, to offer upon His altar, to burn incense, to wear the ephod. Now the Bible declares that Eli kicked at the offering. He did not commit the sin of his sons, but he bore the responsibility of the Temple. The final responsibility was his. Because of the position and authority given to him by God, he should have had greater control over the Temple function and the Temple personnel. He was obliged to protect the integrity of the Temple service, the sacrifice and the priests and any neglect of these duties would be compromise to his call and function. There are many times that the pursuing of our call will mean correction and rebuke to those who are not submitting to the requirements of their service. Without hesitation and delay, they must be brought to accountability. The Temple and its service, the priest and his responsibility represented the highest function on this earth. It must not be treated frivolously or with casualness. The commands and commissions of God must be carried out with alacrity and precision.

Verse 29 gives a holy indictment of Eli's behaviour. Eli was reprimanded by the Almighty for kicking against the offering or scorning the offering or disregarding the deeply significant nature of the offering. This was God's command for His house and the person charged by God to protect and enforce these commands, acted with disregard and disrespect. Remember this was not done in the court square or in the market place. This was done in the Temple. This was the place where God was to be honoured and obeyed and here in the place that was created for His dwelling, the High Priest and his sons dishonoured the Lord. Even though Eli rebuked them, there is no evidence that he stopped their misbehaviour. His sons who stole the choicest part of the sacrifice that was God's, his sons that violated the sacred custom, were never stopped. Please note the action and observe the response. When you are charged with divine responsibility, when you are given the commission by God, nothing and no one must stop you from discharging these responsibilities. Whether you incur the displeasure of the crowd, or the disapproval of the family, you must, you must discharge your God-assigned responsibility. In stopping these men, their lives would have been saved. But much more than this, the Ark would never have been stolen. Here in the Temple, in the house of God, the most grievous sin had been committed. That led to the defeat of the armies of Israel, the death of the priest and the bondage of a nation. It all began in the house of God. The political powers in the world had no power to compromise the Ark. The economic powers had no power to affect the destiny of the Ark. The attacks or opinions of the people had no power to cause the ark to be stolen. It all began in the house of the Lord with renegade priests and an irresponsible High Priest. The Word is fulfilled, "... judgement begins in the House of Lord."

ICHABOD – THE GLORY IS DEPARTED

Samuel 4:17-22 says, *"And the messenger answered and said, Israel is fled before the Philistines , and there hath been also a great slaughter among the people and thy two sons also Hophni and Phinehas are dead, and the ark of God is taken.*

18. And it came to pass, when he made mention of the the ark of God, that he fell from off the seat backward by the side of the gate and his neck brake, and he died: for he was an old man and heavy. And he had judged Israel forty years.

19. And his daughter in law, Phinehas' wife was with child, near to be delivered: and when she heard the tidings that the ark of God was taken, and that her father in law and her husband were dead, she bowed herself and travailed; for her pains came upon her.

20. And about the time of her death, the women that stood by her said unto her, Fear not; for thou hast born a son. But she answered not, neither did she regard it.

21 And she named the child Ichabod, saying, The glory is departed from Israel: because the ark of God was taken, and because of her father in law and her husband. 22. And she said, The glory is departed from Israel: for the ark of God is taken."

The battle between the Philistines and Israel raged and Israel lost. Hophni and Phinehas were killed and the messenger came to give the news to Eli. He, upon hearing the news, fell backward, broke his neck and died. Phineas' wife was about to deliver her child and when she heard that her husband was dead, her father in law was dead and the Ark had been taken, she went into travail. She called the child

Ichabod, for the Glory of God had departed as the Ark was taken. The news of the capture of the Ark killed the High Priest, and so deeply affected was Phinheas' wife, that she named her child Ichabod. Think of the implications of this. This child would be reminded whenever his name was called, that the Glory of God had departed. A family affected a nation in defeat, enemies gloating, all because of the blatant sin of two men and a condoning father. Yes, the failure began in the priesthood and spread to the nation.

CHAPTER 7

Summary

1. The Ark of God, the symbol of His Glory, was taken by enemies. Why?

2. The Ark and the Tabernacle were the centre of the life of Israel.

3. How could the sons of the High Priest be sons of Belial or sons of wickedness?

4. The cause of the departure of the Ark had to do with the priesthood.

5. Because they were close did not mean that they were committed.

6. The sons of the priest violated the laws of sacrifice and incurred the wrath of God.

The High Priest, in not dealing directly and aggressively with the sins of his sons, incurred the displeasure of God.

Chapter 8

The Return of God's Glory

II Samuel 6:1-8 says, *"Again, David gathered together all the chosen men of Israel, thirty thousand.*

2. And David arose, and went with all the people that were with him from Baale of Judah, to bring up from thence the ark of God whose name is called by the name of the Lord of Hosts that dwelleth between the cherubims.

3. And they set the ark of God upon a new cart, and brought it out of the house of Abinadab that was in Gibeah: and Uzzah and Ahio, the sons of Abinadab, drave the new cart.

4. And they brought it out of the house of Abinadab which was at Gibeah, accompanying the ark of god: and Ahio went before the ark,

5. And David and all the house of Israel played before the Lord on all manner of instruments made of fir wood, even on harps, and on psalteries, and on timbrels, and on cornets, and on cymbals.

6. And when they came to Nacon's threshing floor, Uzzah put forth his hand to the ark of God and took hold of it: for the oxen shook it.

7. And the anger of the Lord was kindled against Uzzah; and God smote him there for his error; and there he died by the ark of God.

8. And David was displeased, because the Lord had made a breach upon Uzzah: and he called the name of the place Perezuzzah to this day. "

When David was made king of Israel, he was determined to bring the ark back to where it belonged, in Jerusalem. This is a determination that must be restored to the life of people today. There must be a drive, a hunger, a longing, a determination to see and to experience the Glory of the Lord. Superficial substitutes, liturgy and tradition, programmes and methods that have filled the corridors of many churches, have left God's people, spiritually bankrupt and bereft of power. Much of the church knows about prosperity, deliverance, healing and 10 reasons why you should stay married, 12 reasons for divorce and 14 steps to restoration. Most everything in some churches has been reduced to a formula of some sort, to the neglect of the power of a genuine touch of the Glory of God.

The subject of Glory has become a futuristic, Heavenly, "We will be over there some day," kind of treatment. So many see no relevance of Glory to their lives today. Many have lost the revelation that Almighty God did not touch you and save you to allow you to be blasted by sin, the curse, privation and poverty. He has a supernatural plan for you while you live and He wants to reveal that plan today. This was His powerful prayer in John Ch. 17 where in just a few verses, Our Lord emphasized the glory He gave to His children. This Glory that God gave to Jesus and Jesus gave to His children was a dimension or a realm of all blessing that His children would need. Walking in this dimension, living in this dimension gives access to God's realm that contains the supply to all needs.

Philipians 4:19 states, *"but my God shall supply all your need according to His riches in Glory..."*

In God's realm, there are riches, grace, truth, favour, healing deliverance, joy, peace and a multitude of other things that are vital to our lives. This is the Glory that Jesus has for His people.

Now not only did David possess the determination to bring the Ark back to Jerusalem, He built a Tabernacle to house the Ark. Not only was his position a mental, emotional and spiritual one, he actually did something: he built a place for this Ark to be placed. His was not only the thought and the talk, but the deliberate actions of a man that was ready for restoration. The desire must not end in the thought stage; there must be action, preparation, building and construction. There must be a place that is properly prepared to house the Ark. This is a part of spiritual operation that has been neglected in the church. We ask for so much but are not involved with the preparation for the miracle. Build a place of praise, a place of worship, a place of adoration. Do all you can to encourage the preparation of the heart in worship, the preparation of the mind by the transformation of the Word. Do all you can to prepare the atmosphere with worship, so that the Lord will delight in seeing you receive His Glory.

I Chronicles 15:13 states, *"For because ye did it not at the first, the Lord our God made a breach upon us, for that we sought him not after the due order."*

This verse speaks of seeking the Lord according to His order. I will be speaking of this in detail in this chapter. Many people want the benefits of all that

God has in store but are not interested in being involved in the process. They want the privilege without the responsibility. There must be engagement and involvement before God sends His power or you receive His Glory. You believe, God moves; you ask, then receive; you knock, He opens; you seek, then find; you pray then Heaven responds. There are thousands of instances in Scripture, of the word "If" being mentioned, letting you know that God is ready to do His part if you are willing to do yours. The apathy of so many has lulled them into a sleep that has benighted and blighted their lives.

A PLACE PREPARED

There is a glorious outpouring, a supernatural reception that is ready for you at this moment, but preparation must be made. You do not hear much of the Tabernacle of David but it is mentioned in the Old and New Testaments. In fact in Acts 15:16, we read, "After this I will return, and will build again the tabernacle of David, which is fallen down; and I will build again the ruins thereof, and I will set it up." Yes this tabernacle will be restored. This tabernacle became a place where people would come to offer sacrifices of praise and joy and thanksgiving. Even though this is a future, physical restoration that is being referred to, there is a powerful, personal application today. This speaks of the restoration of praise, worship, adoration that are all transformed into a spiritual building to house His presence. God inhabits the praises of His people or He is enthroned when His people praise Him. He sits on this throne that praise provides, and executes the authority of the King of Kings and Lord of Lords. This is a here and now revelation where your praise, your worship are a vital part of the preparation to house His Glory.

It bewilders me as I travel, to see praiseless Christians that sit as though immobilized, with expressionless faces, drooping hands and a shut mouth. When did it become so difficult to be a praiser and be a worshipper, to be filled with willing expression to the King of Kings. Yes, the devil, formerly Lucifer, knows that your praise prepares for the execution of the authority of the King in your life. The devil does now, all that he can to occupy that throne with fear, depression, anxiety and overwhelming circumstance. He fears your praise, for this praise is what he craves and when it is willingly given to the Almighty, demons tremble. "So tremble on you yapping hounds of hell! For the King sits on my throne executing His Heavenly authority in my life." David prepared a place to house the Ark of the Covenant, called the Tabernacle of David.

MISTAKES ON THE JOURNEY

They are ready to bring the Ark back; the place where it is to be housed is finished. Now the journey begins and immediately there are some major mistakes made. The question would be, how could this happen so early in the journey? I will answer this quickly. II Samuel 6:3 begins by saying that they set the Ark of God on a new cart. This was a Philistine's cart - an enemy's cart was being used to bring the Ark of God into Jerusalem. God will not allow His Presence, His Glory to be ushered in on a Philistine, idolatrous, worldly cart. The Philistines invented the cart, they used the cart and this was the instrument now being used to transport the Ark to Jerusalem. God would have none of it and so was about to abruptly stop this movement. So many in church life are endeavouring to bring in God's presence on a worldly method, or a worldly instrument. These new things invented by the world will never, can never usher in the Presence of God. They may usher in momentary excitement, a substitute touch, but will never, never bring in the precious Presence of Our Lord.

This new cart that had the Ark of God upon it was driven by two men, Uzzah and Ahio. Uzzah means "strength" or the strength of a man. Here, the name of one of the men that drove the Ark had to do with the strength of a man. So here is the scenario. They put the Ark on a new cart, it was pulled by oxen and the two men drove the cart. Animals carried what was supposed to be carried by men. Man was out front directing the Ark. So in essence, they were dictating to God, the direction in which the Ark should have gone. Levites should have carried the Ark on their shoulders but it was on a new cart. Oxen were pulling the Ark and man was doing the driving. Please examine this in the light of what is happening around you so that the same mistakes will not be made. There is no greater honour than to bear the Presence of the Lord. I am not created to carry the oppression and depression that are all around; I am created by God to carry His Glory. So many have taken so little from a God who has so much. How can I complain about the burdens that I carry when what I am called to do is to carry His presence? Is there any greater honour? Is there any more meaningful privilege? Will I give this up to carry the spirit of the world?

STOPPED AT THE THRESHING FLOOR

After this journey had been undertaken, Almighty God put a stop at the threshing floor of Nacon. The Ark is about to come into Jerusalem where the Glory of God would be restored. Before this happens, Almighty God must set up His order for His Glory.

Here at Nacon's threshing floor, the oxen stumbled. The threshing floor is a smooth place and the oxen are the most sure-footed animals. Yet the stumbling took place here. In the smoothest spot, with the most sure-footed animals, there was a stumbling. When this happened, Uzzah stretched forth his hand to steady the Ark and dropped dead next to the Ark. He dared to endeavour to touch the Ark with his hands and there he died. There was stumbling, then there was a shaking. Then Uzzah stretched forth his hand to steady the Ark and died. In II Samuel 6:7, the anger of the Lord was kindled against Uzzah and God smote him for his error. No fleshly hand, no human strength will ever touch the Presence of the Almighty. The Glory of God will not be touched by human hands. Uzzah died next to the Ark that was built to protect life. It was that serious.

The Glory of God, the Ark of God is coming to Jerusalem and before this happens, the programme of man must come to an end. Any parade of flesh, any exhibition of human talent or strength must end. Any method that does not glorify God, any programme that does not point to the Almighty will abruptly stumble. No flesh will glory in this Presence and God's order will be instituted. Man's parade stops here and God's order begins. Let this be your testimony, that no flesh, no human strength or talent will endeavour to be the leading force of your life. God must be the leader, He must be the pilot not the co-pilot. He must be the one in front of my life. "Where He leads me, I will follow," must be the words that guide my everything.

The Tabernacle of David not only occupies a place of profound meaning in the Old Testament, it holds a place of pre-eminence in the prophetic realm and the present realm. In the Old Testament, it was the place the place that was built to house the Ark or the Presence and the Glory of the Lord. Remember David allowed the Ark to be taken to the house of Obed Edom for three months. Obed Edom was not a Jew but this act, prefigured the day when the presence of God, the Glory of the Lord would come to a Gentile bride. The Ark stayed in his house for three months and the Glory of God came to God's people based on Jesus' three day journey of death, burial and resurrection. This three day journey created the birth of the church.

The relevance to the Tabernacle of David for today lies in this truth. When David was dedicating the Temple, 22,000 oxen were slain, 120,000 sheep were slain as sacrifices to the Lord. Today as we live in these fleshly tabernacles, we are asked to offer the sacrifices of praise, joy and thanksgiving. What a magnificent privilege is given to the worshipper of today where we are afforded the honour of offering these praise sacrifices to Our Awesome God!!

CHAPTER 8

Summary

1. David was determined to see the return of God's Glory.
2. He prepared a tabernacle to house the Glory of God.
3. Even though his desire was great, mistakes were made on the journey back to Jerusalem with the Ark.
4. Before God restores His presence, He will restore order.
5. The programme of man must be terminated before the programme of God is instituted.
6. God will not allow fleshly hands to taint His presence.

Uzzah and Ahio died next to the very thing that was supposed to give them life.

Chapter 9

When God Looks Through His Glory

Exodus 14: 21-31 reads, *"And Moses stretched out his hand over the sea; and the Lord caused the sea to go back by a strong east wind all that night, and made the sea dry land, and the waters were divided.*

22. And the children of Israel went into the midst of the sea upon the dry ground: and the waters were a wall unto them on their right hand and their left.

23. And the Egyptians pursued, and went in after them to the midst of the sea, even all Pharaoh's horses, his chariots, and his horsemen.

24. And it came to pass, that in the morning watch, the Lord looked unto the host of the Egyptians through the pillar of fire and of the cloud, and troubled the host of the Egyptians,

25. And took off their chariot wheels, that they drave them heavily: so that the Egyptians said, Let us flee from the face of Israel; for the Lord fighteth for them against the Egyptians.

26. And the Lord said unto Moses, Stretch out thine hand over the sea that the waters may come again upon the Egyptians, upon their chariots, and upon their horsemen.

27. And Moses stretched forth his hand over the sea, and the sea returned to his strength when the morning appeared; and the Egyptians fled against it; and the Lord overthrew the Egyptians in the midst of the sea.

28. And the waters returned and covered the chariots and the horsemen, and all the host of Pharaoh that came into the sea after them; there remained not so much as one of them.

29. But the children of Israel walked upon dry land in the midst of the sea; and the waters were a wall unto them on their right hand, and on their left.

30. Thus the Lord saved Israel that day out of the hand of the Egyptians; and Israel saw the Egyptians dead upon the seashore.

31. And Israel saw that great work which the Lord did upon the Egyptians: and the people feared the Lord and believed the Lord, and His servant Moses."

The parting of the Red Sea remains one of the most outstanding miracles in the Holy Bible. God miraculously provided a path of deliverance for His people and they went through that path. That sea that not only represented, but actually was a prohibitive obstacle, was now an open path for His people to walk through. The Bible says that the enemies pursued, showing the reluctance of the enemy to let these people go. The Israelites had been released but the enemy was still trying to lay claim to them. When you look in your rear view mirror and enemies from your yesterday are pursuing you, be ready for a Divine intervention. So many times when enemies are in hot pursuit, the believer begins to panic and discouragement enters the picture. Please note the following points:

1. Like the children of Israel, you were delivered from the enemies' presence, now you are about to be delivered from their power.

2. To be delivered from their power, their power must be broken beyond question. For the power of the enemy to be broken, the enemies had to die so that their legal claim on God's people would be cancelled.

3. Like the children of Israel, your enemies are behind you, not in front of you.

4. Like the children of Israel, their pursuit to hurt you will turn into judgement for them.

Moses' method of dealing with the enemies of Israel was killing one Egyptian at a time. This human method got him thrown into the wilderness. God's method was to bring them all into the Red Sea so that the song of deliverance would be sung, as it is in Exodus 16. The presence of enemies in your backdrop only testifies of the coming, collective judgement on them. "Yes, you who chase me, you ghosts of yesteryear, come, come all of you to your watery grave!"

Exodus 15:1 says, *"Then sang Moses and the children of Israel this song unto the Lord, and spake, saying, I will sing unto the Lord, for He hath triumphed gloriously: the horse and his rider hath He thrown into the sea."*

Yes, He has triumphed gloriously for this battle continues to be His. Mine is the part of obedience as I faithfully follow His Word and see what He will do. There is a revolutionary point that is made concerning the battle, the enemies, the battleground. People tend to see the enemies through the filter of their own abilities so when the enemies appear, they always seem larger than they in fact are. This is because of the view and the perspective that they are seen from. We feel dwarfed by what confronts us. However, when Almighty God sees the enemies, when He looks at the enemies, the view and the perspective are completely different, the view and perspective are reversed. The enemies are dwarfed before Him. We now must strive to see God's view, God's perspective, the way that God looks at these enemies.

Exodus 14:24 says that in the morning watch, God looked at the hosts of the Egyptians through the pillar of fire and the pillar of cloud. In the Old Testament, the pillar of fire and cloud represented the Glory of God. When God looked at the enemies through these, He was looking at them through His Glory. I said much earlier in this book that we must first live in the dimension of Glory before we emphasize the manifestation of Glory. When God looked through His Glory, manifestation would be automatic since God has no capacity to look at the enemy through anything but His superior, magnificent, Heavenly Glory. The outcome of this is astonishing and filled with relevant revelation for you today. Remember the enemies of the past were in hot pursuit of the Israelites, still claiming that they had a legal right to the life of this nation. It was not enough for Israel to be taken from the presence of Egypt, now Egypt's power, its claim had to be broken.

5 RESULTS OF GOD'S GLORY-GAZE

Exodus 14:24 says that as the Lord looked through the pillar of fire and of cloud, He troubled the host of the Egyptians. These Egyptians that had troubled Israel for so long were now troubled by Almighty God. Let us examine the elements of Pharaoh's bondage over the children of Israel. There were taskmasters set over them. There was a bondage and an enslavement and a godless master that was always wielding the whip over them. These taskmasters afflicted them continuously. Not only were they made slaves, not only were they oppressed by forced labour, not only did they have brutal taskmasters over them, but they were experiencing all the excesses of slavery. The purpose of these excesses was to wear them down so that their resolve, their determination, their drive would be taken away. Then the Bible adds that they were afflicted with burdens. The heaviness of the bondage, the burden of the oppressor, the almost unbearable weight of tyranny all descended upon the Israelites. They built treasure cities for Pharaoh, so all their ingenuity, all their energy was used to build cities for their oppressor and enemy. The thought of enslavement, the thought of forced labour and afflictions that were burdensome, the thought of building cities for the enemy were all a part of their mental enslavement. They were made to serve with vigour and the result was embittered lives. This is the way Pharaoh looked at them and this is how the Egyptians troubled the Israelites. Now, Almighty God looking through His Glory, was about to turn the entire life picture around. Now the enemy was about to see what trouble was, all about.

Think about Exodus 1:12. In bondage the more the Israelites were oppressed, the more they multiplied and they grew. Even in bondage, Almighty God was still with them and the enemies, the Bible says, the enemies were grieved, or the enemies experienced dread, or the enemies became alarmed. All the taskmasters, all the afflictions, all the burdens could not stop the people of God from growing. They were in bondage, yet in the enemies' camp, in Pharaoh's dominion, they grew, they thrived. There was yet a part of them that could not be bound by the enemy. The sovereignty of God superseded their condition and their location. Wherever you are and whatever you are going through, whatever the circumstances are, there is a part of you that Satan has no access to. It is that part of you that will cry out for help for deliverance,

FOR   EXODUS!!!!!

THE CONTINUING MANIFESTATION OF GLORY

The Bible continues in Exodus 14:25 and says that He took off their chariot wheels. The instrument that was being used to transport oppression and attack, was now targeted. Not only would God destroy the enemies but whatever they used, whatever vestige of power was visible, Almighty God went after it to destroy it. These chariots ran on wheels, so the Lord took the wheels off and completely disabled them. You are familiar with the popular saying, "The wheels are coming off." This is the day to notify the chariot that has transported your oppression, your enemies, your threatenings, that the wheels are coming off. Halleujah!!! They must no longer be able to transport this oppressive attack on my life because they are about to lose the wheels. The Scripture continues and says they drave them heavily. When the wheels came off, the chariots began to scrape the ground so that they were literally run into the ground. Here are the mighty chariots of Pharaoh in hot pursuit of God's people, now run into the ground. It is time for a turnaround so that you can see oppressions, satanic instruments that have been used to attack you and run you into the ground.

Now the enemies of Israel that boasted of their strength, their power and their superiority, have a response. In Exodus 14:25 they say that they must flee these marauding warriors, these armies of Pharaoh with their mighty chariots but these soldiers of Pharaoh's court are now fleeing. Fleeing before the awesome power of Israel's God, fleeing from the mighty demonstration of His power. The Egyptians told one another that they had to flee. There needed to be no rebuke or comment from the people of God; these enemies recognized their defeat and admitted this to one another. They recognized their demise and saw their total inability to deal with the demonstration of God's power. When God looked through His Glory, the enemies' power and might dissolved into puniness and irrelevance. This is your time to see enemies fleeing that were once strong and powerful forces that brought bondage and defeat.

Their second response in verse 25 was that the Lord was fighting for them. Whom God chooses, He defends, whom God calls, He preserves, whom God covenants with, He delivers. Remember the Israelites were followers of the instruction of God and in this realm of obedience, the battle is the Lord's.

Exodus 14:13,14 says, *"And Moses said unto the people, Fear ye not, stand still and see the salvation of the Lord, which He will shew to you today: for the Egyptians whom ye have seen today, ye shall see them again no more forever.*
14. The Lord shall fight for you and ye shall hold your peace."

Before they entered the Red Sea, this was the word of God to them. "Stand still, see the salvation of the Lord ... for the Egyptians you see today, you shall see them no more forever. The Lord shall fight for you." All of this was promised before the miracle of the parting of the Red Sea. All they had to do was follow the path of obedience. The Egyptians, when they saw the demonstration of God's power and Glory, they said that the Lord was fighting for Israel. This is another result of God looking through His Glory. When the Ark of the Covenant was in the possession of Israel, no enemy had the power to defeat them. When they followed the pillar of fire and the pillar of cloud, God was always their defence. They followed the cloud, not the crowd. So many today are subtly trapped into following opinion and fads, following the popular and the worldly approved so that they end up on dead end streets. We must learn to follow the cloud, which means we follow the leading of Almighty God. When the children of Israel came to Jericho, the kings of the Amorites and the Canaanites testified of the miracles that had happened to Israel.

Joshua 5:1 says, *"And it came to pass, when all the kings of the Amorites, which were on the side of Jordan westward, and all the kings of the Caanaanites, which were by the sea, heard that the Lord had dried up the waters of Jordan from before the children of Israel, until we were passed over, that their heart melted, neither was there spirit in them anymore, because of the children of Israel."*

News came to them even before Israel arrived and the Scripture says in 5:1 that their heart melted, neither was there spirit in them any more because of the children of Israel. Wow! What a declaration from enemies that were once strong and imposing. The Lord is with them, the Lord fights for them, the Lord is on their side and our hearts melt. We have no force to continue in this battle. This is the testimony of an enemy besieged by the power of God and bewildered by the visible demonstration of His power.

The third response of the enemy was that the Lord fights against us, the Egyptians. He is for them but

He is against us. God is more against your enemies than you are because they are your enemies, opposed to His supernatural plan for your life. The Lord is against the enemies who devise to thwart His purpose for your life. He is against the enemies that pursue you after He has delivered you. Take note that right now, no matter where you are and what you are going through, if you are following this path of obedience, the Lord will deal with your enemies. The Israelites experienced defeat when they lived in disobedience. They experienced bondage when thy lived in rebellion, when they murmured and complained. When they murmured and complained, judgement came among them. But from the moment that they followed God's path and submitted to His plan, His Glory and power were seen.

Now God Speaks to Moses

Up to this point, God looks through His glory and a glorious manifestation of power comes against the enemy. After this, the enemy speaks to one another about this manifestation of the power of God. Now God speaks to Moses to have him cooperate in this miracle. This is of extreme importance for God always purposes to involve His people in the spiritual affairs of earth. He commanded Moses to stretch his hand over the sea so that the waters might come upon the Egyptians, upon their chariots, upon their horses. You may ask why God would do this and involve Moses in this miracle. Remember in a former chapter, we spoke of the prayer of Jesus in John 17. He wanted His people to receive the Glory He had given to them, He wanted them to behold His Glory. His purpose is to involve you in the affairs of His rule and reign. He does not want a detached and distracted people who know nothing of the inner workings of His kingdom. Moses threw down the rod in Pharaoh's court and a miracle happened. He lifted his hands on the mountain and Israel prevailed. He spoke to the rock and water came forth. It is the will of God to bring you in to experience the vital, powerful inner workings of His kingdom. I will show My Glory saith the Lord! Now come and see! Come and experience! Stretch forth thy hand. You are able to stretch yourself to a greater level. Stretch your hand my friend. Stretch your faith! Stretch yourself!

Moses stretched his hand toward the sea that had been a formidable obstacle in the pathway of their deliverance. He is now stretching his hands to that sea where God opened this miraculous pathway. The pathway that was opened would now be shut and judgement would come upon all the enemies. Remember in Exodus 14:16, God asked Moses to stretch the rod and the sea would be opened; now he must stretch his hand and the pathway would be closed. When he obeyed the Lord, every one of Pharaoh's chariots and every one in this army perished. Israel was saved and her enemies judged.

It is an astonishing thought that God would involve you in His Holy operation. It is an amazing thing to know that He is willing to bring us to a place of inclusion in His kingdom's affairs. You can't make a path through the Red Sea Moses, but you can stretch the rod. You can be obedient to follow my word, not disobedient and intimidated by the hugeness of the obstacle. This open pathway of the Red Sea becomes an Old Testament type of the cross of Jesus. It opens up to save and deliver me and shuts in to judge every spiritual enemy, every principality and power. What is the deliverance to God's people, now becomes judgement to God's enemies. He will show His Glory and I get to walk and live in that dimension; He will demonstrate His power and I get to see and participate in that manifestation. Yes all this happens,

"WHEN GOD LOOKS THROUGH HIS GLORY!"

CHAPTER 9

Summary

1. When God looks at your enemies, he looks at them through His Glory.

2. When He looks through His Glory, He troubles the enemies.

3. He drove the chariots into the ground because He destroys the instrument that carried your oppression.

4. He fought for Israel and against the Egyptians.

He included Moses in the miracle and commanded him to stretch forth his hand.

Chapter 10

To See the Glory of God

John 11: 17-25; 38-45 state, *"Then when Jesus came, he found that he had lain in the grave four days already.*

18. Now Bethany was nigh unto Jerusalem, about fifteen furlongs off.

19. And many of the Jews came to Martha and Mary, to comfort them concerning their brother.

20. Then Martha, as soon as she heard that Jesus was coming, went and met him but Mary sat still in the house.

21. Then said Martha unto Jesus, Lord if thou hadst been here, my brother had not died.

22. But I know, that even now, whatsoever thou wilt ask of God, God will give it thee.

23. Jesus saith unto her, Thy brother shall rise again.

24. Martha saith unto him, I know that he shall rise again in the resurrection at the last day.

25. Jesus saith unto her I am the resurrection, and the life: he that believeth in me, though he were dead, yet shall he live:

38. Jesus therefore again groaning in himself cometh to the grave. It was a cave, and a stone lay upon it.

39. Jesus said, Take ye away the stone. Martha, the sister of him that was dead, saith unto him, Lord, by this time he stinketh: for he hath been dead four days.

40. Jesus saith unto her, Said I not unto thee, that, if thou wouldest believe, thou shouldest see the glory of God?

41. Then they took away the stone from the place where the dead was laid. And Jesus lifted up his eyes and said, Father, I thank thee that thou hast heard me.

42. And I know that thou hearest me always: but because of the people which stand by I said it, that they may believe that thou hast sent me.

43. And when he thus had spoken, he cried with a loud voice, Lazarus, come forth.

44. And he that was dead came forth, bound, hand and foot with graveclothes: and his face was bound about with a napkin. Jesus saith unto them, Loose him, and let him go.

45.Then many of the Jews which came to Mary, and had seen the things which Jesus did, believed on him."

These are some of the most illustrative Scriptures in the Holy record so I must deal with them in some detail. Jesus loved Mary, Martha and Lazarus very dearly and a report came to Him that His friend Lazarus was sick. Instead of leaving immediately to come to the rescue of His friends, He tarried in the place where He was. He finally came but by that time, Lazarus was dead and in the grave for 4 days. Jesus was in Jerusalem, only two miles from Bethany, yet Jesus waited to come to Lazarus. When Jesus arrived, Martha came to Him and said, "Lord, if you were here, my brother would not have died." She was living in the past like so many others. If something were different, then outcomes would be different. But the thought of the "What ifs" of the past, never changes the situation of the present.

The present reality was that Lazarus was dead. When Martha said if Jesus were here, that was a glance at the past. That glance at the past, to live in the "What if..." of life, has a negative impact on the present. The name Martha means "bitterness" so it is easy to see that this living in the past would create bitterness in the present. The "What if..." of the past never creates blessing in the present. There are so many that live in the power of their past and discover that there is no future in the past. The only result of recalling the failures, the challenges or defeats of the past, is the instilling of bitterness in the present.

In verse 25, Martha said to Jesus, *"I know that my brother will rise in the resurrection on the last day."*

She displayed great insight into prophecy but this thought was for the future. A few verses before, she was talking of the past, now she is talking about the future. Jesus promptly declares in verse 25, *"I am the resurrection and the life..."* then disregards the past and the future and He declares, *"...I am the life."* My power is in the now, in the present and you are about to see that dimension and that demonstration as you have never seen it before."

TAKE AWAY THE STONE

Jesus is about to show them His Glory and a Heavenly manifestation that would impact this city is about to take place. The atmosphere of Heaven is about to collide with the atmosphere of earth but just before this, we see the divine preamble to this miracle. Jesus addressed the people and said to them, "Take away the stone." Lazarus was dead and they were unable to raise him from the dead. There was a stone in front of the tomb and Jesus would not do what was possible for them to do. If you do what you can, God will do what you can't.

A great miracle from Heaven is about to touch a city and the grave is about to surrender Lazarus. The atmosphere of Heaven is about to collide with the atmosphere of earth and a dramatic manifestation is about to take place. And just before this happens, Almighty God with all His Sovereign power and Supreme Glory involves men and women in the beginning of this miracle. Think about this for a moment. Before the glory of the Exodus, the Israelites had to sprinkle the blood of the lamb on their doorposts. Before the water came from the rock, Moses had to speak to the rock. Before the Red Sea parted, Moses had to stretch his rod out. Before the River Jordan parted, the priests had to take the ark and walk into the River Jordan. At Jericho, they walked around the city and then shouted to the Lord. Whenever there was a great manifestation of God's power, God involved His people and required their obedience to His word. Frustration ensues when people are unwilling to be obedient, when they refuse to be engaged and when they stay stagnant and immobilized. God requires your movement and demands your engagement if you are to see His Glory. If Heaven is to grace you with its magnificent move, if God is to show His Glory, the very least that you can do is to be obediently involved with the commands of God. There are so many that suffer from the disease of ease, they suffer from stagnation and their refusal to move, to become engaged, which robs them of the glories that Almighty God would willingly give. What a pathetic summary, that one could be robbed of such blessing and breakthrough by bowing to the idol of self.

Remember in a previous chapter, I spoke of Moses on Mt. Sinai receiving the law. When he returned, Aaron was leading an idolatry campaign, as they had made for themselves, a golden calf. When Moses descended the mountain, these valley dwellers, these idol worshippers could not look upon him. His face shone with the Glory he had seen on Mt. Sinai and they could not look upon him. The point is powerful; idol worshippers cannot and will not look at Glory. When people bow to false gods, when they worship at the shrines of their puny, pathetic, puerile self-made gods, they inevitably exclude themselves from the awesomeness of God's Glory. Selfish occupations, fleshly attitudes, carnal inclinations, man-made idols of humanism, materialism and hedonism (pleasure) must bow and surrender to the demands of the Almighty.

In the text, they put the stone; now they must remove the stone. The devil did not put it, the people did. So if the people put it, the people could remove it.

Colossians 3:5 states, *"Mortify therefore your members which are upon the earth: fornication, uncleanness, inordinate affection, evil concupiscence, and covetousness, which is idolatry:"*

You are called upon to mortify your members, fornication, uncleanness, inordinate affection, evil concupiscence, and covetousness, WHICH IS IDOLATRY!!! Whatever commands your highest devotion, that is your god. Whatever force the flesh causes to be ascendant in your life is idolatry. So when you hear the statement, I will do what I want, when I want, how I want, you are hearing the very essence of idolatry. This absorption with "I," this addiction to self, this desire for self approval is all a deep form of idolatry. This is a primary hindrance to the reception of the Glory of God. God is not an unwilling God who demands perfection before He gives His gifts. The dimension of Glory is already yours but the hindrance to its reception are the entanglements of the self life. The use of the words, "I, me, mine," has become so frequent that it reflects lives that are dominated by self interest, self inclinations and self absorption. You cannot bow to two gods, you cannot serve two masters. Choose today the puny gods of this decaying world or the awesome Almighty Glorious God of Heaven – Jehovah.

GOD HAS A DIVINE TIMETABLE

This is the second point in the preamble to the glorious manifestation of God's Glory.

John11:14-15 states, *"Then Jesus said unto them plainly, Lazarus is dead .*
15. And I am glad for your sakes that I was not there, to the intent ye may believe; nevertheless let us go unto him.

Jesus said plainly that He did not come at the time that Mary and Martha wanted. I have found that God does not follow my timetable; neither does He follow my calendar. Many times people feel that God's time is not as appropriate as their time. So many complain of the timing of their breakthroughs. Why do I have to go through what I go through to get to where I need to be? Please give me the product without the process. I want the finished car but not the rigor of the assembly line I want the power of the resurrection but not the nails of the Cross or the burial in a borrowed tomb. Give me my breakthrough, my miracle, with no process. If God answered every prayer you prayed, with the timing you required, where would you be and in what condition would you be? God has the aerial view, the view of past, present and future. Jesus waited and when He came to Lazarus' tomb, Lazarus had been dead for four days. In John 1:15, He says I am glad for your sakes that I was not there or in other words, I did not follow your timetable. If it were left up to you, I would have come before Lazarus died but I did not because I had a greater purpose. I tarried so that you would believe, so that the city would be impacted and many would be touched.

Remember in former chapters, in John 17:20-24, He repeatedly talked about His Glory and touching the world. Here in John 11, He says that He did not come just for you and yours, He did not follow your timetable, because the greater purpose was touching the many in Bethany. God's ultimate purpose in raising Lazarus was to impact the people in Bethany. God's aim is always the world. We get trapped by the cares of life and the entanglements of this world. In speaking of Glory in John 17, Jesus mentioned the world twice, letting us know that God's aim in giving you his Glory is not for you to be glorious. The ultimate aim of God in pouring out His Glory, is so that the world will see.

Most times, your idea of proper timing has to do with the convenience of your four and no more. You will see in this chapter, how God connects His Glory to His people and through that connection, touches a region.

BEHOLD HE STINKETH

This is the third element in the preamble to this glorious manifestation that is to come. Jesus knew Lazarus would have been dead for four days, He knew that He would be stinking but still told them to remove the stone. Sometimes God wants for the situation to stink before He shows His Glory and power. If Lazarus was almost dead, human effort might have saved him. But if he was dead, buried and decomposing only God, only Divine intervention, only a miracle from Heaven could raise him from the dead. If this happened, all would have to believe in this Jesus, that His Father was the source and therefore believe on Him. The question must be asked, "Is there a situation in your life that is stinking. Is the stench obvious? Are you feeling dismayed because this scent of decay is all around you?" Get ready for a Heavenly intervention because this was the situation that provided the backdrop for this great miracle. Be not afraid; be not dismayed, Our Lord has arrived to introduce the atmosphere of Heaven. This is where atmospheres collide. The atmosphere of earth is filled with unbelief, fear, decay and death. The atmosphere of Heaven is Glory, power and majesty and life as God knows and experiences it. When Heaven's atmosphere comes in, the atmosphere of earth is pulverized and manifestations of miracles take place. In the grave, there was a stench but in the midst of this foul aroma, a miracle was being prepared.

BELIEVE TO SEE HIS GLORY

The miracle is about to take place and we have been dealing with the elements in the preamble to the miracle. Here comes the fourth element. Jesus spoke to Martha and told her that if she would believe, she would see the Glory of God. Whatever was coming, whatever the nature of the miracle, it was equated to Glory. There are many that have taken themselves out of the realm of Glory by living by the senses. They have to see to believe so they never believe to see. Logic and rationality play the predominant role in their lives. Jesus was telling Martha that the requirement to enter into this Glory realm was to believe. I don't have to deserve this, nor do I have to earn this, but I do have to believe. It is within your power to have faith in God, to believe, OR to live by sight, touch, scent or other senses. In these elements that are the preamble to God's manifestation of Glory, you are only asked to do what is in your power to do.

This move to God is the preamble before God moves to you. The Scripture says in Matthew 11:28, "Come unto me all ye that labour and are heavy laden and I will give you rest." God will give the rest but you have to come to Him. Your move to Him is the beginning of His move to you. You must assume the responsibility for movement, so that you are doing what you can. Before Calvary, God came to people but after Calvary, people come to God and then God comes to people. The death, burial and resurrection of Jesus, provided every possibility for healing, deliverance and blessing. This was God's consummate gift, the gift of the life of His Son and in this death, burial and resurrection, all that Heaven can provide is given to us. Jesus came, Jesus died, Jesus was buried and Jesus rose from the dead. Now that Jesus has done all of this and it is a finished work with finished results, your part is to behave and move toward this enormous heavenly reservoir of Divine provision.

Nothing has the capacity to stop you if you don't want to be stopped. It is a matter of the will. Will you move? Will you defy the laziness of the flesh, the inertia of the world and other false contentment with so little? Your breakthrough is one decision away, for if you believe, if you remove yourself from the sense realm, you shall see the Glory of the Lord. This should be no contest; there should be no hesitation yet so many are stuck in this seductive hold of comfort, complacency and ease. Prayer meetings in church are cancelled, the attendance on Sunday night is so poor, that that too is cancelled and evangelism in the community is all but a past practice. All of this is a consequence of the stagnant state of people and their unwillingness to move with obedience and purpose in God's perfect will. They do enough to have an ease of conscience, they say enough to appease their desires and they hear enough to give them a convenient experience. To them there is no cross to bring death to self and no cost so that their lives remain fixed on personal dreams and ambitions. You ask, "Where is this Glory?" The more accurate question is, "Why are so many content with an earthbound, fleshly, worldly life?

This is a moment of decision that can usher you into a dimension hitherto unknown. Seize this moment, defy the temptation to be satisfied with little, walk in God's dimension and see His Glory.

JESUS LOOKS TO HEAVEN

In John 11:41, when they took away the stone and the condition of death was revealed, Jesus lifted up His eyes to His Father. This is a lesson that must be learned and an example that must be followed. In the midst of the revelation of the death that is before you, your eyes must not be fixed on what is before you but on He who is above you. The atmosphere of earth was that of despair, death and decay. Jesus looked to Heaven for Heaven's atmosphere was about to collide with earth's atmosphere. His ultimate aim according to verse 42 is that they would believe. His interest is the world, the touching of multitudes, not just the blessing of believers. So many churches have lost sight of their true mission, their reason for being and of God's command to them. The church is not a group of people waiting for the next bus to a destination. It is not a club for the elite fleet. It is not a physical edifice to be so ornamented that people gasp at its internal beauty. The church is a group of called out ones that are created to be a witness to the world. This parish is not my world; that world is my parish.

In Israel, the River Jordan begins as three tributaries in Northern Israel. They are called Dan, Banias and Hephzbani. These tributaries are fed by the snowmelt from Mt. Hermon. There are times when the snow is so much that the flow of these tributaries is torrential. These three then flow into what becomes the River Jordan which then flows into two seas: the Sea of Galilee and the Dead Sea. This water in the Sea of Galilee supports all kinds of sea-life but the Dead Sea has absolutely no life. This is astonishing because both seas are fed by the same water. Here is the reason for the condition of both seas. As the Sea of Galilee receives its flow of water, it gives the water but the Dead Sea has no outlet. Anything that is always getting and never giving, soon dies. No matter how powerful the flow, how full of life, if there is no outlet, there will be death. In the midst of all the potential for life and productivity, there is death because there is no giving. May your lives not become a dead sea because of the refusal to be an outlet for God's power and blessing. You are not a reservoir; you are a channel for the blessings of

God to flow to others. From God to you and through you.

This blessing for me and mine, this hoarding of supply is a far cry from God's purpose for your life. God's interest is touching the world and you become the instrument through which that can be done. He will get it **TO YOU** if He can get it **THROUGH YOU!!!** Your glorious beginning as a child of God began because God gave His Son. The nature of God is the nature of love and love is not selfish for it always reaches out to touch those that are around. God gave one Son and by giving that Son, he has received millions and millions of sons. When life changes from a get it all, hoard it all mentality and it becomes a giving, sharing mentality, a spiritual universe of newness fills your life. In this miracle that is about to explode in Bethany, Jesus looked to Heaven.

CHAPTER 10

Summary

1. It is the plan of God for you to see His Glory.

2. Glory is seen in the resurrection of Lazarus.

3. Jesus would raise the dead but He commanded them to remove the stone.

4. If you do what you can, God will do what you can't.

5. Idol worshippers cannot look at Glory.

6. Jesus confronts the stench of the grave and changes it all.

7. God's ultimate goal is to impact the community with His Glory and power.

Glory changes inside and transforms outside.

Chapter 11

Lazarus–Come Forth!!

In verses 42 and 43 of John Chapter 11, Jesus looks to Heaven and speaks to the Father. He is telling the Father that the people around Him need to believe. Here He is, standing before a tomb with Lazarus dead for four days. He is about to bring one of the most glorious miracles in Holy Writ to us. Yet, before He does this, He speaks to His Father. **You must speak to the Father about challenges before you speak to the challenges about the Father.** Jesus did not consult a committee or the human authority, he spoke to His Father. This miracle could not emerge from consultation with flesh and blood. Earth had no power, the leaders could offer no counsel, no advice that could have brought Lazarus from the grave. There are some things that will be so dead, so decaying, so putrid that only Heaven, only Almighty God has the power to change them. Before you speak to the problem about God, speak to God abut the problem. No vote, no board discussion, no committee conclusion could bring this man back from death. Let it be known today in the midst of all that is happening, I look to the Father which is in Heaven and I speak to Him. Jesus was speaking to His Father about those around Him who would believe because Almighty God had sent Him. In His mind, this demonstration of Glory was not just a way to demonstrate His Power or to enhance Himself, but to touch the world. This is a point that needs to be understood by God's people. Demonstrations of Glory are not brought to enhance your reputation. They happen so that those around you are touched by the power of the Almighty.

Now Jesus speaks to Lazarus!!!
"LAZARUS, COME FORTH!!!"

Remember, Lazarus is dead, he is already in Paradise which at this time was in the underworld. Paradise was not yet translated to the heavens. So when Jesus said, "Come Forth!" His voice, His authority thundered not only in the grave but in the underworld. This word of authority pierced through this world into the other world, into eternity and commanded Lazarus to come out, come up and come forth. No human voice, no human effort could even think of speaking to Paradise to surrender one of its occupants. This would take someone that had supreme power in three worlds, Heaven, earth and the grave, the underworld. This would call for the ultimate demonstration of God's Glory as He called forth Lazarus. And Lazarus came forth! Oh death, where is thy sting, oh grave where is thy victory. The underworld had to surrender its hold because Heaven's dimension took over. Jesus equated this resurrection of Lazarus to a demonstration of His Glory. He told Martha if you believe, you will see the Glory of God and she did.

RESURRECTED BUT BOUND

And the dead came forth, Lazarus came forth BUT He was bound. He was out of the hold of death, out of the grasp of the grave but he was bound hand and foot with grave clothes. This was in addition to the miracle where he arose from the dead. He was bound with the bindings of the graveclothes yet he was able to walk out of his grave. These bindings did not matter in the grave, these grave clothes belonged to the grave, but when he was raised, this clothing had to be removed. Clothing of the past, the bindings of the grave, the embalming of the dead has no place in the resurrected life. Even though he was out of the grave because of a magnificent miracle, there was still an element of bondage upon him.

There are so many that can declare, "I am saved, I have come out of the grave of sin." But yet, bindings of the grave, clothing of the past still form bondages on their lives. Lazarus' hands were bound and his face was bound. Hands could not move. He could not walk around and he could not see or hear. Sounds like a condition in many lives today. Hands never lifted to God or reaching out to the world; feet never walking in Godly paths; eyes that are bandaged over so that there is no vision and ears that covered up so that they don't hear the word of the Lord. There are so many that have the bondages of the past upon their lives but Jesus is about to give an important instruction.

Jesus said to them, "LOOSE Him and let him go!" There is now, enormous life flowing in this man. "Loose him, let him go, let him be free to go to places that need that life." When he is loosed, he must go. Immobility and stagnation are no longer a part of his life. This is another message for those in the church today. You are loosed to go. You are not loosed to be lost in a maze of apathy and inactivity. You are loosed to help to bring loosening to others. Lazarus had to preach no messages of resurrection for he was a living example of God's power to resurrect. There is amazing Heavenly life in this man but he is bound. He is unable to express that life to its fullest degree.

Even though the miracle is that he is out of the grave, the continuous expression of that miracle demands that he be loose. Whatever is on the inside must be expressed outwardly but this expression is impeded when there are bandages and bondages.

LOOSE HIM AND LET HIM GO!!!

The implication of these words is that if he is not loosed, he cannot go and all of this Glory, all of this Resurrection would be for him alone. Power is not given for you to be powerful but for you to be a witness. The Glory of God is not manifested for you to declare, "I have seen manifestation." It is given so that the world will know who Jesus is. This is one of the areas of real concern to me in the body of Christ.

Whenever there is some manifestation of Glory and we must be sure that there is, some people would take that manifestation and make it the only way that God can move. They make a movement out of the move. It is all about their localizing the move or placing the Glory of God into a manifestation mould. Then, these people that have done this feel that this specific manifestation must be repeated over and over and without it, there is no Glory. My question is, "What impact does this have on the on-looking world. I am in no way opposed to manifestation that the Glory of God creates by its immediate impact, Heavenly manifestation. But we must remember that Glory is first a dimension, Heaven's dimension and as this dimension moves in, the atmosphere is changed and manifestation flows. I become particularly concerned when the manifestation becomes the end and there is little understanding of dimension. It is like Peter, James and John on the mountain of Transfiguration.

John 17:1-8 states: *"These words spake Jesus, and lifted up His eyes to heaven, and said,*
Father, the hour is come; glorify thy Son, that thy Son also may glorify Thee:
2. As thou hast given him power over all flesh, that he should give eternal life to as
many as thou has given him
3. And this is life eternal, that they might know thee the only true God, and Jesus
Christ, whom thou hast sent,
4. I have glorified thee on the earth: I have finished the work which thou gavest me to
do.
5. And now O Father, glorify thou me with thine own self with the glory which I had
with thee before the world was

6. I have manifested thy name unto the men
which thou gavest me out of the world:
thine they were, and thou gavest them me;
and they have kept thy word.
7. Now they have known that all things
whatsoever thou hast given me are of thee.
8. For I have given unto them the words
which thou gavest me; and they have
received them and have known surely that
I came out from thee, and they have
believed that thou didst send me."

As eternity was temporarily rolled back and they saw Jesus transfigured, His face shone like the sun, and His raiment was white as the light.

3 TABERNACLES

They saw His Glory and then Moses and Elijah appeared. Peter then said that it was good for them to be there so that they should build three tabernacles, one for Moses, one for Elijah and one for Jesus. While he was yet speaking, a bright cloud overshadowed them and a voice out of the loud spoke and said, "This is my beloved son in whom I am well pleased, hear ye Him." This record in John 17 bears amazing parallels to this discourse. When they saw

His Glory, when they saw the manifestation, their first response was to build three tabernacles. Let us build because we have seen a manifestation but there were some flaws in their desire to build. The first was the desire to build three tabernacles, one for Moses, one for Elijah and one for Jesus. Here where they saw Jesus in a way that they had never seen Him, they wanted to give Elijah and Moses the same treatment that they were going to give to Jesus. They would place Moses and Elijah on the same level as Jesus and give to them, the same homage. Immediately, a voice came out of the cloud and said, "This is My beloved Son, hear ye Him." Here Jesus alone is to be adored and heard. No other, no matter how sterling the reputation or how profound the manifestation, no one must be placed on the same level as Jesus. In my opinion, many times the manifestation takes the place of Jesus.

The disciples said in John 17:4 that it was good for them to be there. There is that "my four and no more" mentality. Right after they said that it was good for them to be there, they said, *"Let us make here three tabernacles."* I suggest that this building had a touch of shrine-building about it. Let us make, let us erect a tabernacle to remember this manifestation but they included two men with Jesus. It is a clear and present danger in church life when people become shrine builders. They erect these structures to self, to their gifts, their abilities and they actually structure God out by their man-made designs. You never put any man, regardless of the wonderful gifts that are invested in him, ever, ever on the same level with Jesus. This becomes filled with an element of idolatry and any monument built around this, becomes shrine building. To display God's feeling about this suggestion to build, even while they were speaking, God spoke from the cloud. Heaven interrupted their fleshly tirade and said, "This is my beloved son in whom I am well pleased, hear ye Him." I will have you hear the voice of no one or follow the voice of no one. I have just shown you My Son in a way you have never seen him. How could you put any other on His level? Can you equate any other to Jesus? Who is like unto Thee? The Heavenly tone was so overpowering that when they heard His voice, they fell on their faces and became afraid. This response was wonderful because they fell on their faces before the Lord.

HIDE THE FACE

In His presence, In His Glory, there must be a bowing. The 24 elders and the 4 living creatures around the throne, praise, worship and bow. This is the scene in Heaven and it must be the scene on earth. This bowing indicates submission, humility, reverence and adoration. It would be a wonderful thing if there were more bowing in church life as we are grasped by the Holy Glory of the Almighty. They fell on their faces because where the Glory of God is, only the face of God must be shown. This happens around the throne of God as the seraphim hide their faces with two wings. There must be no human showiness, no human exhibition in the place where God's Glory falls. Knees bent and face hidden, are the appropriate response to the descent of God's Glory.

In verse 6, it says that they were afraid. Would to God that people who have built structures or shrines, people who have put others on the same level with Jesus, become afraid. It is a fearsome thing to endeavour to touch the Glory of God. This was seen with great clarity when Uzzah touched the Ark and fell dead. In the dimension of His Glory, in the atmosphere of His Glory, the human print must be eradicated; showiness of the human face must be hidden. Attitudes of human reliance and independence must be eradicated in this place. No flesh must glory in His presence. After all of the manifestations, when all the emotion had settled, they lifted up their eyes and saw no man, except Jesus alone. This is a wonderful testimony that must be internalized by the believer. No man must be in the sights of the believer; it must be Jesus alone. There are so many visible distractions that dominate the sight, the vision of the believer. Eyes placed on circumstances, eyes placed on man all become major distractions, major obstacles to spiritual growth. Jesus must occupy the place of pre-eminence in you and around you.

CHANGED AND TRANSFIGURED

In II Cor.3:18, the Bible speaks about being changed into that same image. In Matthew 17:2, the Bible speaks about being transfigured. In these two scriptures, the word changed and the word transfigured are the same words in the Greek language. It is the word *metamorpho* which means outward change. Our English word metamorphosis is derived from this and is associated with the process of a caterpillar becoming a butterfly. It includes the emphasis on outward change. Most times we associate the Glory and change to inward conditions and this is a great part of the change. But there is also another element of this change that is essentially outward. Remember in John 17:20-24, the world has to be impacted. In John 11, the community must see. The world cannot see the heart so God has included an external manifestation of Glory. Remember the face of Moses shone after the Sinai experience and in Matthew 17:2, Jesus' face shone like the sun and His raiment was white as light. There are times in my life when people who never knew me would say to me, that there was something different about me. Others would say that I looked different. This has happened to many of you and this represents that external touch of the Glory of God.

In Matthew 17:1, Jesus brought them apart to a high mountain to show them His Glory. You must come apart before you come apart. If you don't come apart in separation and rest, you will come apart and unravel in chaos. God will take you to a high place, apart from the maddening rush of the world, apart from the consistent influence of circumstances, apart from the entanglements of life, and show you His Glory. The world will endeavour to keep you in its grip, to hold you with the demands that surround you, to bind you and grind you. In staying in this place, you will eventually come apart emotionally, mentally and spiritually. "No man that warreth, entangleth himself with the affairs of life," says the Bible. Jesus brought them apart to a high place and showed them His Glory. Before the cross, before the burial, resurrection and ascension, they saw Jesus with the physical veil pulled back and they caught a glimpse of eternity. It is your turn now.

Come apart! Do not be caught! Do not be trapped!!!!

CHAPTER 11

Summary

1. The ultimate demonstration of Glory was the resurrection of Lazarus.

2. Even though Lazarus was raised from the dead, he was bound and had to be loosed.

3. The disciples were asked to loose him because God will never do the possible.

4. He was loosed to be let go, not loosed to be lost in activity.

5. Glory has a transforming effect on people as seen in Moses and Jesus.

6. Jesus delayed his appearance in Bethany so that the Glory would be seen by all.

God's ultimate purpose is to see the community, the region and the world impacted by the power of God.

Conclusion

I have said many times in this book that God's ultimate reason for the demonstration of Glory is to touch the world. Many feel that this Glory is to be claimed and possessed by the church and the final results are the manifestations in the church. No! No! No! The church is only the conduit so that this Glory can flow and touch the world. Many in church have claimed ownership of this Glory and have said that this is the only way Glory is to be seen. God is never interested in the labels of the people or the definition by the people. When Lazarus arose, it was the ultimate manifestation of the Glory of God but it did not stop there. In John 11:43, the Scripture says that many Jews believed on Him. Hallelujah for this manifestation of His Glory. Some of them went to the Pharisees speaking of the miracle. Religious powers must be notified that Jesus has come in His Glory and power. They convened a council and said that this man, if He is left alone, all men would believe on Him. Now these were the unbelieving Pharisees that were saying that if Jesus were allowed to continue, all would believe on Him. This miracle, this demonstration of Glory had a dramatic impact on the community and the religious world. The impact was so dramatic that from that day forth, they took counsel to put Him to death. They had no response to the Glory of God and to the manifestation of His power. They could not stop people from believing because of the greatness of His touch.

It is my prayer that the content of this book has opened up a little more understanding about His Glory, His dimension and His atmosphere. There are things that are within your power to do, that if done, will open the door to the glorious and the miraculous. This is your moment to see a transfiguration in your life and to see impact all around you. You will see His Glory and atmospheres that are around you that bring worldly fear, doubt and defeat will be pulverized,

When Heaven's Atmosphere and Earth's Atmosphere Collide!!